TURKANA

Other books by Nigel Pavitt

Kenya: The First Explorers

Samburu

TURKANA

KENYA'S NOMADS OF THE JADE SEA

Nigel Pavitt

Designed by Barney Wan

Harry N. Abrams, Inc., Publishers

First published in Great Britain in 1997 by The Harvill Press, London

Library of Congress Cataloging-in-Publication Data
Pavitt, Nigel.
Turkana : Kenya's nomads of the Jade Sea / Nigel Pavitt.
p. cm.
Includes bibliographical references and index.
ISBN 0–8109–3896–0 (cloth)
1. Turkana (African people) I. Title.
DT433.545.T87P39 1997
967.62'7—dc21   97–7568

Copyright © Nigel Pavitt, 1997
Maps © The Harvill Press, 1997
Jacket Design by Julio C. Bravo

Published in 1997 by Harry N. Abrams, Incorporated, New York
A Times Mirror Company
All rights reserved. No part of the contents of this book may be
reproduced without the written permission of the publisher
Printed and bound in Italy by Amilcare Pizzi S.p.A., Milan

 Harry N. Abrams, Inc.
100 Fifth Avenue
New York, N.Y. 10011
www.abramsbooks.com

HALF-TITLE PAGE: A young man looks out over Lake Turkana. The remarkable jade colour is caused by green algae with high chlorophyll concentrations. It is one of the oldest and largest lakes of Africa's Great Rift Valley system, and the biggest in Kenya.

TITLE PAGE: A man strides purposefully across the Lotikipi Plains watched by an Egyptian vulture atop a termite mound. The Uganda Escarpment is visible in the far distance. Most Turkana believe the world is flat. They know little about the land beyond their own, other than it is *akwap a emoit* (the land of the enemy).

RIGHT: In the early morning, a Turkana with his traditional fishing basket waits at the shores of Lake Turkana for friends to join him before fishing the shallow waters for tilapia (*Tilapia nilotica* and *Tailpia zillii*), types of bream which are delicious to eat. Many pastoralists in East Africa adopt a one-legged stance when relaxing.

Euphorbia shrubs growing among black basalt boulders. Extensive lava flows are a conspicuous aftermath of Pleistocene volcanic activity at the southern end of Lake Turkana near Sirima. Curiously, the boulders which make walking a perfect misery, remain warm to the touch until late into the night.

Acknowledgements

THIS BOOK COULD not have been written without the help and enthusiasm of a large cross-section of Turkana to whom I owe a great debt of gratitude. They gave me a fascinating insight into their way of life and usually tolerated my camera despite beliefs among some of them that photographs remove a part of their soul, making them vulnerable to disease. My special thanks are due to Father Bernhard Ruhnau and his nomadic community, Emekwi Nalukoowoi, Isaiah Ekidor, Francis Lokidongoi and Ome Longori. I am also indebted to the Provincial Commissioner, Rift Valley Province in whose province the Turkana live.

Many people have been generous with information on the Turkana and ideas for my research. I owe much to Susan Southwick for her enthusiastic assistance with my draft manuscript; Dr Anthony Barrett for sharing with me his knowledge of Turkana customs; Dr Meave Leakey for her comments on the prehistory of the region; Bob McConnell for his information of the lake and its resources; Halewijn Scheuerman of Jade Sea Journeys for a memorable boat trip on Lake Turkana; and Susanne Morrell and Vicky Chignall for their useful comments and suggestions.

Barney Wan has been a great help to me in selecting photographs, and putting together a sequence that accurately portrays the people, their customs and the environment. It has been a pleasure working with him.

Finally, I must acknowledge the unfailing support of Michael Towon who accompanied me on all my safaris to Turkanaland. His assistance in camp and with cooking, driving and vehicle maintenance, and as an interpreter in times of need was invaluable to the successful completion of this book.

Author's Note

MOST COUNTRIES AND many places in the East African Region have been renamed this century. I have used the names that were in common use at the particular period of history I have covered in my text. The one notable exception is Lake Turkana which I have referred to as such throughout the book to avoid confusion.

Contents

LEFT: Dancers perform the song of the bulls. The men jump high in the air to demonstrate the fierceness of their favourite ox.

Much of the heartland of the Turkana is desert or semidesert terrain with scant rainfall. During the long dry seasons, unremitting winds whip up the loose, sandy soil into terrific duststorms. Powerful gusts also stir up swirling dust devils which career out of control like giant smokestacks across the open plains. They add to the never-ending process of erosion in a forbidding landscape that can be miraculously transformed into pastureland in a year of bountiful rain.

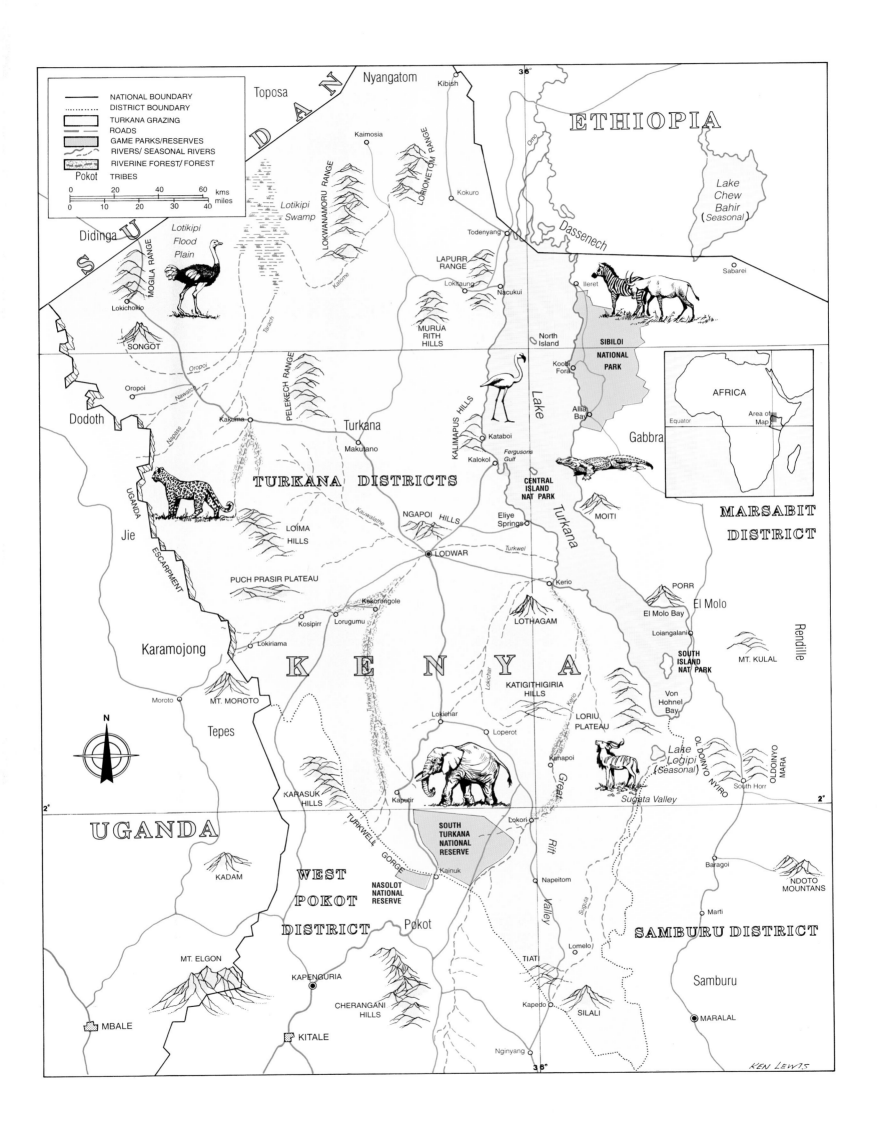

Legend

——————	NATIONAL BOUNDARY
....	DISTRICT BOUNDARY
	TURKANA GRAZING
	ROADS
	GAME PARKS/RESERVES
	RIVERS/ SEASONAL RIVERS
	RIVERINE FOREST/ FOREST
Pokot	TRIBES

kms 0 20 40 60
miles 0 10 20 30 40

SUDAN

Toposa
Nyangatom
Kibish

ETHIOPIA

Didinga
Kaimosia

Lake Chew Bahir (Seasonal)

Kokuro
Sabarei

Todenyang
Dassenech

Lotikipi Swamp

LORIONETOM RANGE
LOKWANAMORU RANGE

LAPURR RANGE

Lotikipi Flood Plain

MOGILA RANGE

Lokichokio

Lokitaung
Nacukui
Ileret

SIBILOI NATIONAL PARK

SONGOT

MURUA RITH HILLS

North Island

Koobi Fora

Tarach
Oropoi

PELEKECH RANGE

Kalome

KALIMAPUS HILLS

Lake

Allia Bay

AFRICA

Equator

Area of Map

Dodoth
Oropoi
Nawata
Kakuma

Turkana

Katoboi

Fergusons Gulf

Kalokol

CENTRAL ISLAND NAT PARK

Gabbra

MARSABIT DISTRICT

Makutano

TURKANA DISTRICTS

Kauwalathe

NGAPOI HILLS

Eliye Springs

Turkana

MOITI

UGANDA

Jie

LOIMA HILLS

ESCARPMENT

PUCH PRASIR PLATEAU

LODWAR

Turkwel

Kerio

PORR

El Molo

El Molo Bay

Rendille

Kekorengole

Kosipirr
Lorugumu

LOTHAGAM

Lokichar

Loiangalani

Karamojong

Lokiriama

K E N Y A

Katigithigiria Hills

SOUTH ISLAND NAT PARK

MT. KULAL

Moroto
MT. MOROTO

Loperot

LORIU PLATEAU

Von Hohnel Bay

Tepes

Lokichar

Kanapoi

Lake Logipi (Seasonal)

OL DOINYO NYIRO

OLDOINYO MARA

South Horr

KARASUK HILLS

Kaputir

Lokori

Suguta Valley

2°

UGANDA

TURKWELL GORGE

SOUTH TURKANA NATIONAL RESERVE

Kainuk

Napeitom

Great

Baragoi

NDOTO MOUNTAINS

KADAM

NASOLOT NATIONAL RESERVE

WEST POKOT DISTRICT

Pokot

Rift

Suguta

Marti

SAMBURU DISTRICT

MT. ELGON

KAPENGURIA

Lomelo

Samburu

MBALE

CHERANGANI HILLS

TIAT

SILALI

Kapedo

MARALAL

KITALE

Nginyang

3 6°

KEN LEWIS

INTRODUCTION

TURKANALAND LIES JUST north of the equator in northwest Kenya, with Ethiopia, the Sudan, and Uganda on its borders to the north and west. Almost the size of the Republic of Ireland, and representing twelve per cent of Kenya's land mass, it is divided into the administrative districts of Lodwar and Lokitaung. Both districts are wholly within the Great Rift Valley, the world's most formidable geological fault, a great scar that runs north–south for 2000 miles through eastern and central Africa. Here, amid the punishing heat and rocky terrain of one of the harshest regions of Africa, landscape is on a grand scale.

The region is sparsely populated by the Turkana, the largest ethnic group of the Ateger-speaking people, an eastern Nilotic cluster of seven tribes. Roughly 350,000 strong, they are one of the last truly nomadic peoples of Africa. Fortunately for the Turkana their land is too remote and too dry to interest outsiders. Governments elsewhere have taken the traditional territories of their own nomads to settle ever-increasing general populations. As skilful stockmen with an intimate knowledge of the local flora, for generations the Turkana have extracted a living from land that is for the most part as inhospitable as the Sahel.

I visited Turkana District, as it was known then, for the first time in 1957, when I was a young army officer. After driving for two hours from the prosperous European farming area of Kitale, I stopped at a police road barrier. A large notice board announced: TURKANA DISTRICT. ENTRY STRICTLY FORBIDDEN. The Closed Districts Ordinance prevented anyone entering the area without a permit issued by the relevant provincial or district commissioner. Officials in such closed districts were very powerful.

A few miles beyond the police post, a rough, twisting track descended 2000 feet to the Turkana country below. At the top, another sign prominently displayed a skull and crossbones, and warned PRIVATE BURIAL GROUND FOR RECKLESS DRIVERS. Later I learned that several speeding army lorries in years past had plummeted over the edge.

I remember wondering how people and livestock could survive in the Turkana wilderness. The low-lying plains extend to endless horizons embracing sand, stone and rock. In some Turkana areas the ubiquitous thorn bushes grow well; in others, vegetation is sparse desert scrub protected by a mantle of vicious prickles and spikes. Even the grass is perniciously spiky. Trees are few and form a dusty green fringe along the main *luggas* (seasonal water courses). Permanent homesteads are scattered, and stock is constantly on the move in search of feed. Towards the end of a gruelling dry season, all looks undernourished: people, livestock and plant life.

Two-thirds of northwest Kenya is inhospitable semidesert. Within this area, the administrative centre of Lodwar is a sprawling frontier town. Strong easterly winds blow with exhausting monotony, whipping the sand into terrific dust storms which blot out the sun for days. Residents call the stinging dust 'Lodwar rain', for they hardly ever see the real thing. The annual pittance averages less than six inches a year and is often half that amount.

Some of the Turkana's best grazing grounds are near their unsettled northern and western borders, which are prone to attack. In this region, jagged hills and rugged mountain massifs thrust up in savage splendour from the surrounding plains. The steep-sided Uganda Escarpment, a conspicuous geographical feature, marks

LEFT: Herds of Turkana cattle cross the El Barta plains toward a seasonal water pan. After rain, the plains provide important grazing for the Turkana, Samburu and Rendille pastoralists.

Turkana warrior, 1888

the northernmost extension of Kenya's Central Rift system. Forming the western boundary of Turkanaland, it is also the international border between Kenya and Uganda. Living 2000 feet higher in Uganda, the Karamojong, Jie, and Dodoth speak the same language as the Turkana. However, the Karamojong and Dodoth have warred constantly with the Turkana since they went their separate ways after pushing up the Nile some three hundred years ago to settle in East Africa.

The climate of the distant mountains is influenced by the highlands in Uganda and southern Ethiopia, and good rains often occur. The peaks and plateaux of the largest mountains are forested and provide essential refuge for cattle in times of drought.

The Lotikipi in the west, is a dry flood plain for much of the year. Strangely in such an arid area, parts of it become a true swamp from the flood waters of the Tarach River in heavy rain. In the very distant wetter past, it linked Lake Turkana to the Nile. Today, the environment is daunting. It is, I think, one of the most uncomfortable places I know, becoming like a furnace at midday.

The Lotikipi spills over the Kenyan border into southeast Sudan. There the Turkana clash frequently over grazing and water rights with more of their Ateger-speaking neighbours, the Toposa and Nyangatom. Earlier this century, Britain concluded a border agreement between her Uganda Protectorate and Anglo-Egyptian Sudan without considering ethnological issues. The Boundary Commissioners abandoned their difficult task in the Mogila mountain range before completing a thorough survey of the eastern extremity, and drew a straight line on the map. With the stroke of a pen, the Turkana lost important dry weather grazing to the Sudan. This included an area known as the Ilemi Triangle which is inaccessible for much of the year to the rest of the Sudan. It has always been *de facto*, if not *de jure*, a part of Kenya and administered as such. In real life, the locals take no notice of invisible lines created by unreliable mapmakers. The place has always been a melting pot of tribal friction where temporary occupation is constantly challenged. Today, spears and shields are replaced by Kalashnikov AK47 assault rifles, often used to deadly effect.

Lake Turkana forms the eastern boundary of Turkanaland. It is Kenya's biggest lake and the sixth largest in Africa. The lake is surrounded by exceedingly barren, windswept lands, yet has a spellbinding attraction. Lying scarcely 1200 feet above sea level, its vast expanse of water is tinged emerald green and can be breathtakingly beautiful in the light of early morning or late afternoon.

Two large seasonal rivers, the Turkwell and Kerio, meander through Lodwar District, and are a lifeline which supports an ever-increasing static population. The rest of the region is unsuited to farming, for the soil has poor fertility and rainfall is very unpredictable: it may fall in one area and miss another close by, and vary considerably from year to year. Daytime temperatures soar above 100° F in the shade with little change at night. The prevailing southeasterly winds can be incessant, and their drying effect immense. Most rain falls during the *akiporo*, the only wet season. It ushers in a time of plenty which may last from April until July. The short October to November rains are usually spasmodic and poor.

As the dry season ends, the smell of rain on the tinder-dry golden grass is something that lingers long in the memory. The wind stills, the heat haze clears as the temperature drops, and the countryside takes on its own rare beauty. The grey aspect of the dormant acacia scrub changes within days to an iridescent green. Trees burst into leaf, the birds, butterflies and bees take on a new urgency in life, and the parched earth becomes a carpet of verdant grass dotted with wild flowers.

The origins of the Turkana are legendary throughout the tribe. The tale recounts how a very severe drought ravaged Jie country about two hundred years ago. Many people died of starvation, and the herds were decimated. Those who survived split up to forage in different directions.

An old woman called Nayece is said to have lost her husband and most of her relatives. In desperation, she bravely descended the steep-sided escarpment bordering her homeland into the uninhabited, low-lying country beyond the foothills. Soon, she found trees and bushes laden with all types of edible fruits and wild berries. She was alone, but decided to stay for a while beside a hill situated a short distance from the Tarach River, now known as Moru Anayeche (the hills of Nayece). There, she gathered and dried as many berries as she could find to feed members of her family left behind.

One day when out foraging, she came across a lone bull grazing near the banks of the river. She realized it must have strayed from Jie country and drove it to her temporary shelter where she tethered it to a tree. Each day, she grazed and watered it before setting out to gather more berries. Within a short time, it became extremely fat.

Meanwhile in Jie country, eight strong, young men were despatched by the elders to look for the stray, a prized animal with a distinctive bluish-grey coat. Tracking it down the escarpment was easy, but the spoor became extremely difficult to follow on the flood plains near the Tarach. The bull had wandered aimlessly and numerous wild animals had crossed its tracks. The young men were further baffled when they saw a set of human footprints alongside the spoor. After days of frustration crisscrossing the countryside, they heard a cow lowing in the distance and hurried to investigate. In a while, they stumbled upon their bull being tended by Nayece. They were amazed at how much food she had gathered and decided to rest for a few days to regain their strength. Days turned into weeks and weeks into months, and they were still undecided about when to return home.

Turkana girl, 1888

The elders in Jie worried over the disappearance of their young men and eventually despatched another group of eight warriors to search the area. Upon seeing a land of plenty and Nayece's food reserves, they too decided to relax for a few days. After endless debate, both groups reasoned that the best way of helping their starving relatives was to persuade them to migrate. The young men returned home and put their case eloquently to their people, but the elders stubbornly refused to countenance a move into unknown territory. The younger generation liked the idea, however. They drove their families' herds down the escarpment, ignoring the furious reaction of the old men who shouted and cursed them, wishing them misfortune wherever they went.

After a time, it dawned on the elders that the young people had taken too much stock. A band of able-bodied men was sent to retrieve the cattle. When the two groups met, the young men adamantly refused to part with a single animal. A scuffle ensued in which lives were lost. The old men despatched other groups, but the young men were defiant in defence of their herds and sent word to the elders that they would never acquiesce to such a preposterous demand.

This story may explain the Turkana's traditional friendship with the Jie and their age-old enmity with the Karamojong. *Kara* means 'dying' and *mojong* means 'old people'. So the people who stayed behind and tried to snatch most of the livestock were the Karamojong. This feeling of bad blood gave rise to a century of vicious raids and counter-raids solely to steal cattle. The name 'Turkana' is derived from *Ng'iturkana* which means 'the cave dwellers'. There were a number of caves in the hills near Moru Anayece where the young people settled. It did not take them long to use that name for themselves.

While remarkably similar tribal tales are fairly common in Africa, there is no doubt the Turkana did split from their Ateger-speaking cousins and move east – probably at the turn of the eighteenth century. Beyond one hundred years oral tradition is often confused making it difficult to differentiate fact from fiction. It is unusual, therefore, that the story of the Turkana's origins is so widely known. This does not mean that they grew out of these Genesis-like beginnings. Traditional stories and different dialects support a diversity of origin.

As the Turkana moved down the Tarach, they came to realize they were not alone in the region: fires could be seen burning at night on the distant hills. They met 'red' people who herded strange animals akin to 'giraffes with humps on their backs'. These strangers were the Rendille who daub themselves with red ochre and are still great camel owners. They also came across remnant communities such as the Siger who owned long-horned black cattle; they were assimilated, but maintained their identity by becoming a territorial section within the tribe.

*Warrior with
scarification, 1888*

The Turkana are divided into eleven major territorial sections, each with several sub-groups. Stock watering rights are based on these sections and there are some minor differences of dress. Otherwise, they are not as significant as the thirty to forty divisions within the tribe founded on animal brands. Every Turkana also belongs to one of two moieties which are based on colour. The *ng'irisae* (leopards) are the yellow division while the *ng'imor* (mountains) are the black. A son will take on at birth the opposite moiety to his father; the only exception is an illegitimate boy who takes the opposite to his maternal grandfather. Women belong to the same moieties as their husbands and wear different coloured metal wedding necklaces. Other than meat feasts held on ceremonial occasions and certain peculiarities of dress, the two divisions have never been important. However, they were once a quick and useful method of splitting a raiding force into two when the need arose.

The Jie may have made the Turkana's expansion possible by giving material support. In times of drought, they supplied sorghum and grain; and more importantly, in times of conflict, they provided the Turkana with spears and wrist knives made from local iron by the Labwor blacksmiths of Western Karamojo. Before or during this era of unhindered growth, the Turkana acquired hump-backed zebu cattle which are much hardier than the humpless breeds of earlier pastoralists, since they require less water and grazing. Perhaps the story of the lost bull is allegorical, alluding to this cattle acquisition, a vital prerequisite to Turkana occupation of the inhospitable terrain between the Uganda Escarpment and Lake Turkana.

In the middle of the nineteenth century, a picture emerges of the Turkana as a virile, supremely confident people moving into sparsely populated territory, and assimilating scattered communities as they went. With no tribal hierarchy to lay down strategy or military leadership to control and influence, the expansion was generally fragmented and achieved without much opposition. Yet, by the end of the last century, no other tribe in East Africa except possibly the Maasai, was so feared and so destructive. They had assumed a life founded on raiding, but unlike the Maasai, coexisted at home without serious internal strife. There were good reasons for the change.

Foremost was the emergence of a remarkable diviner named Lokerio whose supernatural predictions brought him to great prominence. The Turkana believe their diviners are the personal representatives of Akuj, their God, with whom they commune in their dreams. Akuj is the supreme being and creator of all things past and present who controls the climate, especially rain. He lives in heaven surrounded by huge herds of cattle which feed contentedly on evergreen pastures. Though usually benevolent, he is quite capable of punishing wrongdoers.

Every Turkana turned to Lokerio for wisdom and guidance. A man of dynamic personality, he was able to instil a sense of pride in his people and create a tribal identity where none had existed before. As his fame spread, he usurped the traditional authority of the elders since their influence rarely extended beyond their immediate family circle and friends. In so doing, he harnessed exuberant young men into a much larger and more dangerous military machine. Turkana expansion turned into aggression and stock rustling corrected the unfortunate circumstances of having been born poor.

The Turkana were also increasingly hostile to foreigners whose behaviour left much to be desired. A motley collection of freebooters flocked to the Turkwell in the 1880s when word spread that the riverine forest had the finest elephant hunting left in East Africa. They intrigued with the locals, then cheated them, thereby bringing insecurity and lawlessness to a fragile area. The Turkana tolerated the scoundrels for their inexhaustible supply of coveted trade goods, but also had their revenge. By day they sold the intruders livestock to ration their porters, but by night they stole the animals back. If a shot was fired in anger, stragglers would be speared in retaliation. The warriors were fearless and contemptuous of 'the Arabs' who fired wildly in the air. Most of these 'Arab' traders were actually coastal Swahilis with some Arab blood.

The Turkana were very successful at trapping elephants to supply the burgeoning trade. Women scraped and pounded giraffe hide for several days before twisting it into a stout rope the thickness of a hawser. One end of it was tied round a deep notch cut into a heavy tree trunk which could be carried with difficulty by ten to twelve men. The other end was fitted noose-like around a circular piece of wood slightly larger than a full grown elephant's foot. Into this a mass of sharpened staves was fixed to meet in the middle. This snare was placed carefully in a well-used game trail. A hole was dug two feet deep and the diameter of the noose. The hunters then concealed it with a covering of soil and leaves. If an elephant trod in the trap, the impetus of its body tightened the thong round its foot, thus impeding movement in the thick bush until it could be safely dispatched.

Man with sack-like hairstyle, 1888

In 1888, Count Samuel Teleki, a Transylvanian aristocrat, and Lieutenant Ludwig von Höhnel, a young Austrian naval officer, became the Turkana's first visitors from Europe. They received a reasonably friendly reception from the Turkana when they crossed the Loriu Plateau at the south end of Lake Turkana, and camped beneath the shade of flat-topped acacia trees lining the Kerio River:

> . . . the camp was filled with Turkana of every age, and these people being the very noisiest we ever met with, the wood soon echoed with their shouts, whilst the way in which a dozen warriors advanced to greet us resembled the charge of an enemy rather than the peaceful welcome we knew it to be meant for. With uplifted spears and shields . . . they sprang towards us, hiding behind every bit of cover as they came, to dash out again the next minute . . . . After these preliminary contortions, however, the warriors squatted down and quietly waited for a present.

Teleki made a costly error in failing to include tobacco in his huge inventory of trade goods. It gave him his first insight into the difficulties of dealing with tribesmen who were used to getting their own way. The situation to them was quite straightforward. Either the visitors produced tobacco – it mattered not from where – or they were wasting everyone's time negotiating to buy cattle no matter how much pleading they did. To this day, no other gift is so universally desirable. Wisely, Teleki did not force the issue, but others following him were not so tolerant, especially when faced with starvation.

Almost seven years elapsed before anyone else from Europe visited Turkanaland. Then, as interest in the largely unexplored region grew, a series of expeditions set out in quick succession. The first two were hunting trips. Arthur Neumann, an English hunter who had started out from Mombasa, arrived at the southern extremity of Lake Turkana on 6 December 1894 while Dr A. Donaldson Smith, an American, travelling from the east, struck the north end of the lake on 14 July 1895. Neither of them had serious problems in their dealings with the Turkana but nor did they venture far into the hinterland.

Successful expeditions always prepared for the worst. Captain H. H. Austin, an officer of the Royal Engineers, who commanded a column of a major expedition to the Nile, unwisely underestimated the difficulties of obtaining resupplies on the march. Having led his men up the largely unexplored west side of Lake Turkana with thirty-seven days' rations, he took for granted there would be an abundance of food at the Omo Delta. So confident was he that he commandeered donkeys en route for carrying the extra loads. Instead, he found the villagers starving. Armed Abyssinians on horseback had plundered their settlements several months previously. Some people were so hungry, they had tied leather belts tightly round their stomachs to stave off the pangs. The column was in a precarious plight as Austin took the only course open to him and retraced his steps along the lakeshore.

The military had grown accustomed to making no provision for livestock because it was anticipated that ample supplies would be captured as soon as an expedition entered 'enemy' territory. With death from starvation becoming more likely every day, and the Turkana deliberately keeping their distance, Austin seized their unattended flocks on the Turkwell with the intention of forcing them to sell the expedition 220 sheep and goats. Though professing a willingness to trade, their reaction was immediate and ferocious, demonstrating how formidable they were when provoked. Volleys of gunfire did not deter their pugnacious spearmen from charging time and again into Austin's ranks. His diaries give a vivid account of the difficulties he experienced because of this cynical miscalculation. Travel in Turkanaland was never the same again.

1

A History of Strife

T HE FIRST ACCOUNTS of nineteenth-century travellers and explorers to East Africa encouraged the European colonial powers to indulge in an undignified scramble for new territory in the region's little known interior. Britain and Germany were the principal protagonists and benefited hugely from the Anglo-German Agreement of 1886. This protocol divided the area into neat spheres of influence by arbitrarily drawing straight lines on a map. By then, Britain had staked her claim to large tracts of land. She did so because the Suez Canal was the life-line of the British Empire, and whoever controlled the headwaters of the Nile controlled Egypt and the canal. The colonial machinations of France and Belgium made Uganda of major strategic importance to Britain, and the compelling reason for her to declare a protectorate over it in 1894. Its ill-defined borders encompassed the whole of Turkanaland, which was still unchartered territory. The British East Africa Protectorate came into being a year later on 1 July 1895 and was somewhat smaller than the Kenya of today.

Five years after the Anglo-German accord, Italy ceded to Britain all the southern part of Abyssinia below a line drawn through the 6° north parallel. (Abyssinia was not generally called Ethiopia until the country was liberated from Mussolini's Italy in 1941.) Strangely this land was not a part of Italian Somaliland, and Italy had no jurisdiction over it. Emperor Menelik II of Abyssinia fumed: 'I do not intend to listen quietly when governments from foreign lands say they will divide up Africa.' He was adamant that the 'effective occupation' of his empire ran south of Lake Turkana. In a fit of pique, he later claimed an extra 7000 square miles of territory south to the Wei-Wei River, at the foot of the Cherangani Hills.

Though treaties were signed settling the Abyssinian/Somali and Abyssinian/Sudanese frontiers between 1897 and 1902, Menelik stubbornly resisted every attempt to demarcate his southern boundary. Eventually, he was put under such sustained pressure by Captain John Harrington, the first diplomatic representative from Britain to the Emperor's court, that he was forced to relent. By then, the British lion had become somewhat uneasy about the territorial ambitions of the Lion of Judah.

The Turkana knew nothing of these imperial designs. They carried on their lives just as they had always done, defending their herds and raiding beyond tribal boundaries with as much freedom as their forbears. Explorers added their sketchy observations and reported each other's rumours as fact. Traders portrayed the Turkana as treacherous, aggressive and insolent to protect their valuable sources of ivory. Captain Montague Wellby, who led an early expedition through Abyssinia to the Nile, added to the illusion. He contended that the Turkana were a race of giants, estimating the height of the men he saw at seven feet. Actually, he did not have much contact with them because they were frightened of his retinue of Abyssinian porters and fled the caravan for fear of being taken into slavery. Sir Harry Johnston, the Special Commissioner and Commander-in-Chief for the Uganda Protectorate at the turn of the century, embellished Wellby's story by depicting them as 'the tallest race living on the globe's surface'. Turkana men went about perfectly naked in those days. With ostrich feathers stuck into their unique chignon-style hairdos, they possibly appeared much taller than their real height.

More misguided notions circulated when the fledgling British administration at Baringo first came into contact with the Turkana in 1903. Living in a fortified station, H. Hyde-Baker, collected tax and administered 10,000 square miles of Queen Victoria's new domain. One day he received an unexpected delegation of Turkana,

LEFT: A Commiphora tree struggles for survival in a confused jumble of lava rocks. Basalt lava fields are a feature of southern Turkanaland.

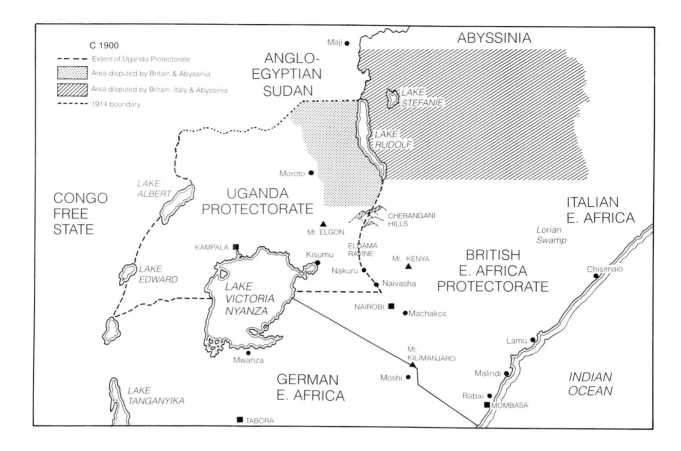

all of whom were said to be over six feet three inches tall. They had come, supposedly, to warn him of their intention to demolish his station and kill everyone inside. They never returned to carry out their alleged threat but it gave the collector and his men many sleepless nights! It seems that Hyde-Baker's interpreter was so scared coming face to face with these notoriously warlike people that he took fright and invented the story. Much later, it was suggested that the delegation had come to seek the collector's help against marauding bands of well-armed Abyssinians. Understandably, the request fell on deaf ears. The Turkana saw no further need to cooperate with the British administration. Had they received help, they might have come to view British intrusion very differently. As it was, when the Collector made his first official visit to southern Turkanaland in 1905, he was met with open hostility. This set the pattern of relations between the two sides for almost two decades.

When Uganda's eastern province was transferred to the British East Africa Protectorate on 1 April 1902, responsibility for Turkanaland was split between the two territories. While Uganda refused to allocate funds to administer the largely unexplored north, the authorities in Nairobi made some attempt to introduce law and order south of the Turkwell River. One of their first decisions was to ban the sale of cow ivory to conserve the dwindling herds of elephants. Since Abyssinia did not follow suit, the outlaws, freebooters and exploiters operating north of Mount Elgon judged the time had come to flee north where they could continue to enjoy a completely free hand in their indiscriminate slaughter of game.

Abyssinia was unruly and its citizens rendered scant obedience to the orders of their own government. The treaties and agreements signed in Addis Ababa meant nothing to officials on the ground. Far away at Maji, a frontier base 100 miles north of Lake Turkana on the Kibish River, the provincial governor continued to operate very much in his own way. Under his patronage, Arabs, Swahilis and Baluchis set up shop and turned the seedy place into a thriving centre for the ivory trade where all kinds of guns and ammunition were sold in full public view.

The renegades operated with impunity from Abyssinian soil for the first two decades of this century. With border warlords, they systematically hunted the great herds of elephants roaming the Turkana and Karamojong plains. Menelik gave them his wholehearted support because he needed to barter ivory for magazine rifles to re-equip his troops. Menelik also urged his provincial governor to destabilize the region by encouraging the Turkana to pillage and poach. This suited the governor, for his principal source of income came from ivory and tax he levied on the local populace.

Until the boundary between Uganda, the British East Africa Protectorate and Abyssinia was finally settled, the Turkana were caught between opposing imperial nations competing for a rugged tract of wilderness. That it was Turkanaland was immaterial to those involved in the power struggle. Abyssinia was more influential because the Commissioners of the two British Protectorates had no wish to squander manpower and money on subduing the inhabitants of 'barren wastes'. Abyssinia even appointed a governor of northern Turkanaland who continued in office until 1918 – fully a decade after the limits of her southern boundary had been finally and irreversibly agreed.

One intractable problem facing the first British administrators in East Africa was the unrestricted sale of arms and ammunition. By the late nineteenth century, the situation was out of hand with many firms in Zanzibar and elsewhere making huge profits from the trade. All the early importations were cheap iron flintlocks and muzzle loaders. They were not made to last, and rusted quickly in the coastal humidity.

Importation of precision weapons was much more serious. Between 1874 and 1878, all the major European powers re-equipped their armies with breech-loading rifles. A couple of years later these weapons became obsolete as the higher performance magazine rifle was introduced. This rapid improvement in technology resulted in good quality firearms being discarded and sold in world markets. Up to 100,000 per annum entered Africa through East African ports. Merchants overcame the ban imposed under the Brussels Treaty of 1890 by shipping consignments outside the limits of prohibition to Muscat where they were hidden in dhows, the wooden sailing ships of the region, destined for Zanzibar.

France also flouted the ban by shipping new Le Gras magazine rifles to Djibouti, the seaport of French Somaliland which was her only colony in East Africa. While the bulk of these firearms re-equipped Menelik's vast armies to spite arch colonial rival, Italy, some were 'secretly' reshipped to ports down the east coast of Africa in dhows flying the French Flag for protection. The dhow captains acted with impunity because at the Brussels conference France would not agree to her vessels being searched at sea.

By 1902 Djibouti was linked by rail to Harar and increasing quantities of rifles filtered down to southern Abyssinia and into Uganda. The Turkana were quick to realize that men armed with rifles had at their mercy the cattle and possessions of neighbours armed with spears. They wasted no time accumulating their own arsenal, ten cattle or one large or two small elephant tusks buying a rifle with forty rounds of ammunition. Loose ammunition was sold at three rounds per pound of ivory.

Other than the Nandi of Kenya, the Turkana were the only tribe in East Africa actively to resist British rule for any length of time. The British tactic of mounting systematic and thorough punitive operations aimed at expropriating their livestock under the Collective Punishment Ordinance was heavy-handed and one-sided. Instead of being cowed into submission, the Turkana became irreconcilable and determined to oppose alien laws and policies which were never explained or understood.

The British also failed to understand other aspects of the rough justice of punitive expeditions. The Pokot and Karamojong invariably exaggerated claims of looted livestock. This meant that the Turkana's herds were confiscated as well. It was not merely this injustice that caused the Turkana to rebel. Most expeditions recruited armed levies to help sequester and drive the captured stock. For operations in Turkanaland, it is hard to imagine, even with the benefit of hindsight, why they were recruited from the ranks of the Turkana's inveterate enemies who had long since had avaricious designs on Turkana cattle. The authorities were naïvely unaware of this intrigue, and misjudged the upsurge of tribal feeling after the 'theft' of the Turkana's prized herds. Men lived for their cattle, and were fully prepared to die defending them.

The Turkana adduced from Britain's failure to follow up punitive expeditions with effective administration that raiding was the white man's sole objective. The British became notorious as the biggest cattle thieves they had ever met, in cahoots with their enemies to loot Turkana wealth. Colonial policy was to protect the tribes which were well disposed to protectorate governments irrespective of circumstances on the ground. Prompted by self-interest, the weakest always sided with the British as a means of defence against the strong. While Britain believed the Turkana needed a firm hand to check dissent, heavy material losses for the Turkana actually upset the balance of tribal power and caused conflicts to escalate.

From 1908 onwards, there was a growing realization in government circles of the need to pacify the disaffected north. However, it came at a time when Whitehall was reducing grants-in-aid and pressing colonial governments to balance their meagre budgets. Also, white settlers were appointed to the Legislative Council, the mainly unelected parliament in Nairobi. They lobbied the executive to curtail military expenditure in the north of the country since it was sufficiently vast and desolate for Abyssinia and the Turkana not to pose a threat. They saw no moral duty to protect the border tribes from outside aggression if they had to foot the bill. A policy was formulated to contain the Turkana, not administer them, which made a mockery of their status as British protected persons. If the Turkana felt threatened by this short-sightedness, they did not show it.

With raids continuing unabated, two offensives were launched, the first in 1914 and the second a year later. They resulted in the death of more than 400 tribesmen and the confiscation of huge quantities of livestock. At least 20,000 head of cattle and 100,000 sheep and goats were rounded up, robbing many innocent people of their very means of survival. The animals not slaughtered to ration soldiers and government employees were distributed as bounty to chiefs and tribes loyal to the protectorate governments. However, the operations failed to capture the outstanding Turkana war leader, Ebei. Also, by targeting the mainly unarmed southern Turkana, the few communities friendly to the British were alienated. This triggered an exodus to the well-armed, more warlike northern Turkana. Ebei's standing among his people rose as word spread that the British were cowards, willing only to confront spearmen. As if to prove a point, Ebei unleashed a fresh round of stock raids to recover the 'stolen' herds. In a three-month period, 15,000 head of cattle were retrieved.

Even in an emergency, military action could not be taken swiftly. The wild northern country was still unsurveyed, and the Turkana assiduously avoided showing foreigners water points and the easiest routes through their land. Their silence was so complete that incidents could take place right under people's noses without anyone ever knowing. Maps of the area were vague and misleading; blank spaces were filled with imaginative and unhelpful legends such as 'Nomad Tribes, Treacherous' and 'rolling hills, dry except during rains'. However, the most difficult problem was the logistical nightmare of keeping a large force supplied on the ground with long lines of communication which had to be guarded constantly. In contrast, the Turkana were extremely mobile. Indifferent to fatigue and suffering, they could walk up to fifty miles a day and survive on practically nothing.

At the conclusion of the second offensive, the Governors of the Uganda and the British East Africa Protectorates — the post of commissioner had been restyled governor in 1906 — met in Nairobi to hammer out a new strategy for 'administering' the Turkana. They conceded that a division of responsibility between the two protectorates and the *laissez-faire* attitude previously adopted had proved singularly unsatisfactory. Yet, neither of them showed any enthusiasm for shouldering the burden. Despite the lack of any formal agreement to realign the interterritorial boundary, the authorities in Nairobi were prevailed upon to administer the entire tribe because lawlessness in the north was a potential threat to the security of white settlers in the East Africa Protectorate. This group was economically and politically too powerful to be ignored.

To test British resolve, Abyssinia became more openly and aggressively involved in Turkanaland. For the first time, government outposts and mobile patrols were targeted to the astonishment and alarm of those in charge. Britain made strong protests in Addis Ababa after which the Emperor called upon his provincial governor at

Maji to account for his actions. Meanwhile, preparations were put in hand to mount another punitive expedition.

Variously called the 'Turkana Patrol' and the 'Labur Patrol' (Mount Lapur, a prominent mountain just north-west of Lake Turkana, was one of Ebei's strongholds), the 1918 offensive brought together the biggest force ever to assemble in East Africa for the purpose of subduing one tribe. Though the military outcome was not as successful as the field commanders had hoped, it marked a turning point in the pacification of the region; it also marked a turning point in the bitter rearguard action Abyssinian officials at Maji had fought for control of Turkanaland and its lucrative ivory resources.

If, as seems likely, the fundamental purpose of the offensive was to starve the northern sections into submission, it was very effective. In isolation, the loss of 350 men and the seizure of several thousand head of cattle was not a serious blow to the tribe providing that stock losses could be recouped by time-honoured, traditional means. This had always been possible in the past because there had been no funds for a permanent garrison to patrol the border. Britain's failure to administer and protect her citizens was the crux of the entire problem. The Turkana would not have posed a particular threat to law and order had they not been given succour and armed with modern weapons by Abyssinia.

The belated measures Britain took to bring the region under proper and permanent control left the audacious Turkana no longer able to plunder their enemies' herds with impunity. In consequence, those families, whose live-stock had been confiscated arbitrarily, faced great hardship. In a cruel twist of fate, the offensive was succeeded by a punishing drought which reduced the proud people to desperation and famine. Indeed, the catastrophic stock losses, following so soon after sequestration, had such a terrible affect on the tribe's economic base that its resistance to foreign intervention was finally broken. Many of today's problems stem from early misfortunes and colonial mistakes.

From the outset of British rule, the Turkana had no cause to appreciate the advantages of 'good' governance. They hated alien cultures being thrust upon them and were riled at new legal systems and new religions which were contrary to their tribal beliefs. The British judicial system was particularly abhorred since custom required no action against wrongdoers unless the victim's close relatives demanded it. No one could understand why the killing of an adulterer or a witch was treated as murder when death by spearing was then, and is still considered to be entirely justified. Similarly, the British judged the slaying of a man in a stock raid as murder, which was nonsense to people permanently on a war footing.

Top civil servants in Nairobi agonized over how best to administer the Turkana. At last, they had come to realize the district was not sufficiently pacified for a rudimentary civil administration to operate effectively. The people were quite simply too unruly. With considerable reluctance, a decision was made to turn the district over to the military, which some viewed almost as a defeat. The early administrators had tried hard but were over-whelmed by the task. From the beginning, they had found it difficult to glean information from the locals who mistrusted anyone not a Turkana. When a district commissioner wished to visit them, word passed rapidly from homestead to homestead that he was in the vicinity, and everyone promptly decamped with their herds. After an all day trek in the sweltering heat, he would be lucky to find a homestead or two occupied. As dusk approached, he would have to return to his heavily guarded camp. The next day the area for miles around would be utterly deserted. This aggravating little tactic was most successful in forcing him to pack up and go home.

In 1919 Captain Eric von Otter was put in command of the Turkana military administration and improved relations immeasurably with the locals. Of Swedish nobility, he was known to his fellow officers as *Risasi moja* (one bullet) for his superb marksmanship with a sporting rifle. He was answerable to both the Uganda and British East Africa Protectorate governments which led to bureaucratic wrangling on the vital issue of funding. In spite of this, he exercised his authority with flair and imagination, succeeding in unfavourable circumstances when others had failed. He went out of his way to learn the Turkana language since he appreciated the need to communicate effectively. To his lasting credit, he avoided the preconceived prejudices that had wrong-footed his civilian predecessors. Having a sensitivity to the rights of the people, which was rare in those days, he punished only those who were proved to have done wrong.

Within a year, he had gained the grudging respect of most Turkana elders by persuading the Governor to vary an unjust confiscation order for 30,000 head of their cattle. He also tackled the intractable problem of Abyssinian cross-border raids. He and a group of energetic young officers brought the place firmly under British authority and paved the way for a civil administration to resume jurisdiction over the Turkana in 1926. Concurrently, Uganda relieved herself of her neglected Rudolf Province by ceding it to Kenya. (The East Africa Protectorate came to an end and the Colony and Protectorate of Kenya was born on 31 December 1920.) To begin with, the district was divided into two, Northern Turkana with its headquarters at Lodwar and Southern Turkana with its headquarters at Kaputir. After seven years or so, they were amalgamated into one district again.

The district commissioner based himself at Lodwar which was still an insignificant outpost of the British Empire. His residence and office were situated on an outcrop of volcanic lava overlooking the Turkwell River (an anglicized corruption of *tirrikwel*, meaning something permanent) and consisted of makeshift buildings constructed of mud-bricks, baked hard in the sun. Because of the heat, they had neither doors nor windows. Besides there was no theft. A handful of other ramshackle buildings completed the post. The buildings were guarded night and day by tribal policemen, the district commissioner's small private army of Turkana braves. Selected for their magnificent physique, they were a sight to behold on parade. They wore all the finery of their tribe with bandoliers of polished leather across their bare chests. Their only clothing consisted of short blue loin-cloths; these had red borders and 'TD' sewn in large red letters in front.

The disarming of the Turkana was a contentious issue. Enticed by Abyssinia, the northern sections of the tribe had accumulated an arsenal of at least a thousand modern rifles. The colonial governments in East Africa saw themselves as agents of civilization and viewed disarmament as a vital prerequisite to the establishment of law and order. Senior officials had a deep-seated notion that the Turkana were the worst aggressors. If the tribesmen were disarmed, peace would reign. Nothing could have been further from reality in such a volatile region. Britain should have learnt from past experience the dangers of meddling piecemeal in the balance of power. By the time the Turkana had been forced into unilateral disarmament, their enemies were ready to strike. Like vultures poised to swoop on prey, the Pokot, who called the Turkana *punyoonik* (the enemies with long noses), wasted little time before attempting to settle old scores. Similarly, the Dassenach, better known until recently as the Merille, armed themselves across the border in Abyssinia to plunder the Turkana herds. Being truculent instigators of trouble, the Merille had the backing of local Abyssinian officials, who soon realized they could replace the Turkana as proxies for imperialism.

The authorities in Nairobi sat back and dithered. It took them eight years to establish a forward patrol base of the King's African Rifles at Lokitaung to protect the citizens they had rendered defenceless. In those intervening years the Merille attacked ferociously, and in 1924, killed Ebei in a rout of the northern territorial sections. Though the British had come to admire him for his bravery, they were relieved that he was dead, for he had been outspoken in his opposition to colonial rule. His death was a terrible blow to the Turkana, whose remnant forces, pacified and largely disarmed, were unable to prevent the Merille raiding further south than ever before. Sadly, the one administrator who had built confidence and trust with the people, was dead. Von Otter had died of blackwater fever the year before Ebei was slain and had been buried by his comrades in full military uniform in a doum palm grove at the foot of Lodwar cone. He had achieved more in five years than had all his predecessors put together in the previous twenty.

The Merille have been a continual thorn in the flesh of the Turkana. They were rearmed with new Italian rifles and trained in guerrilla tactics soon after Mussolini's army invaded Abyssinia in 1935. They never lost an opportunity to use those weapons to good effect against their disarmed neighbours. At the outbreak of World War Two, the British raised a small force of Turkana irregulars to spy on enemy troop movements and help defend the

Sack-like hairstyle made of plaited hair. The tight-fitting necklace is brass. 1919

Elder with black ostrich feather headdress, nose-plate and painted body markings. 1920

frontier against a possible Italian advance on Kitale. Having been lectured for years on the importance of good neighbourliness, the Turkana were incredulous at the white man's double standards when it came to 'their' war. Nevertheless, they were delighted to cooperate because it offered them an opportunity to revenge themselves on the murderous Merille. It turned into a phoney war with few casualties on either side. At the end of it, the Turkana were disarmed. The Merille were not.

Hairstyle in which a gourd stalk decorates the clay bun. 1930

I went to Turkanaland in 1957 to protect the Turkana after a series of particularly bloody raids. As usual women and children had borne the brunt of the slaughter with a few old men speared and emasculated. I was stationed with my *askaris* (soldiers) for five months at Todenyang where the Public Works Department had just built a fine fort on the site of the one which had been destroyed during the war. Our source of fresh water was the Omo River in Ethiopia, where I lost more blood to mosquitoes than any other place I have been. The Merille lived there, and sang and danced until the early hours of each morning because the mosquitoes prevented them retiring earlier. They carried their rifles openly, but nothing could be done to disarm them unless they crossed the invisible border onto Kenyan soil. It was a frustrating game of cat and mouse; as soon as we withdrew to barracks 500 miles away, they attacked again.

Throughout the years of British rule, Turkana district was cut off from the outside world due to the Closed Districts Ordinance. This resulted in the people of northern Kenya being isolated from the rest of the country for forty years. Civil servants were not even allowed to travel by lorry on the main roads between 15 April and 15 June and again between 15 October and 15 December each year because of the rains. The restriction applied whether it rained or not!

This legislation did more harm than good because it made the northern tribes feel they were being treated differently. Education and medical facilities were denied, and development lagged behind the rest of the country. Though missionaries were at the forefront of improving these facilities in other parts of Kenya, they were kept out of Turkana district until 1956, when the African Inland Mission, an interdenominational Protestant group, opened a station at Lokori. Red tape and religious rivalry prevented Catholic missionaries gaining access to the district until 1961.

Tribal policeman, with an ivory lip ornament and leather bandolier. 1955

Being so remote, little effort was made to develop Turkana district. Instead, its remoteness was put to good use as a detention centre for Mau Mau detainees in the 1950s. The most prominent among them was Jomo Kenyatta, who became the first President of the Republic of Kenya. It was he who repealed the ordinance in 1964, though its regulations remained in force for several more years. He also encouraged development, for he had experienced first-hand the negative aspects of enforced isolationism.

The Turkana entered the 1960s barely touched by the benefits and disadvantages of the twentieth century. Other than the partial cessation of stock raids which had been the principal occupation of their young men, they still practised a way of life that had remained unchanged for generations. People's lives were dictated by the timeless rhythm of the rains, not the vagaries of modern man. Even a money economy was despised. Due to the ravages of termites, notes were not accepted as tender, only coins which they never willingly exchanged among themselves. Since then many things have changed – many for better, but others for worse.

A rare sight of three klipspringers. These small antelopes have dainty, rounded hooves, suitable for the rocky terrain in which they live. It often seems as if they watch the approach of strangers standing on tip-toe.

RIGHT: A typical scene on the east side of Lake Turkana. It is amazing how goats survive in these inhospitable lands. Arid and semi-arid lands make up three-quarters of Kenya, but only support a quarter of the population, for nature imposes harsh controls on the carrying capacity of the land.

Songot Mountain stands dark and forbidding in a rare rainstorm. Situated in the west of the district, it has important dry weather pasture on its upper slopes.

LEFT: Turkanaland lies between 1200 feet and 2000 feet above sea level and is one of the driest regions in East Africa. From the air, *luggas* (seasonal river courses) seem to be damp tendrils clinging precariously to sandy wastes. Rainfall runs rapidly off the barren soil, sometimes causing flash floods.

ABOVE AND RIGHT: A Turkana homestead in the foothills of Mount Nyiru.

An aerial view of the southern end of Lake Turkana which is named Von Höhnel Bay after the Austrian naval officer who accompanied Count Teleki on his epic journey of exploration and discovery in 1888. The perfectly formed cone of an extinct volcano juts into its jade waters and is called by the Turkana *Naboi eetom*, the elephant's stomach. The place is still exactly as the two explorers found it one hundred years ago.

As the midday sun stokes up the searing heat on the Lotikipi Plains, the land begins to shimmer. Then, mirages appear and faraway objects play freakish tricks on one's eyes. A flock of goats 'floats' past a homestead with a surreal tree-lined watercourse behind.

A view from Lokichar of acacia thorn scrub, and jagged mountain ranges rising to the south of this important trading centre.

On arrival at a new homestead site, women erect a temporary shelter for their children with donkey panniers and hides, using a framework of pliable sticks.

LEFT: A woman returns home balancing on her head a load of acacia thorn scrub, which she will use to fence the stock pens.

Millet is grown close to the banks of the semipermanent rivers in the district. Children have to guard the ripening crop from baboons and quelea birds (*Quelea quelea*), voracious grain feeders whose numbers can reach locust-like proportions. *Wimbi* or millet (*Eleusine coracana*) was the first grain to appear in the region and probably came with migrants up the Nile many centuries ago; maize made its appearance much later from India. In a bountiful year, women, who are almost entirely responsible for agriculture, can harvest four crops of millet from the same plants and patch of land.

RIGHT: There are no permanent rivers in Turkanaland. The Kerio, which rises far to the south of the district, is one of the most important seasonal water courses. It has belts of thick vegetation and large stands of acacia trees which provide essential dry season refuge for people and their stock.

A pretty young girl has already had a hole pierced in the flesh below her lower lip into which an ornament will be placed after her marriage about the age of fifteen. The rims of her ears have also been pierced and the holes kept open with small wooden sticks. As a married woman, she will insert into each either small brass rings from which will hang tiny circles of polished goat horn or leaf-shaped metal pendants. These earrings vary in number between four and eight, depending on family tradition.

LEFT: A herdsman watches over his camels watering at the Turkwell River, a semipermanent watercourse that is a lifeline for pastoralists living in arid Central Turkanaland. Maize, millet and bananas are grown along its banks. The distant Karasuk Hills are where the Pokot, traditional enemies of the Turkana, live.

A distinguished Turkana elder. His hairstyle and ivory lip plug identify him as coming from west Turkanaland. Note the metal wire protruding from his bun. He uses it to kill lice which often get into the hair under the clay during sleep.

LEFT: A young girl adorned with necklaces of a style the Southern Turkana prefer to wear.

Both sexes from youth to old age love chewing quids of local tobacco or grinding it to take as snuff. They eject saliva frequently through a gap in their teeth to punctuate a conversation, emphasize a point or merely as a sign of conceit. Most people have their two lower incisors removed in childhood which originated as a life-saving precaution against lockjaw; milk could be poured into a victim's mouth through the gap which helped him or her to survive the ghastly locking effect of the bacterial disease. These days the affliction is extremely rare but the custom persists.

LEFT: An old Turkana medicine man. His wooden necklaces are charms to ward off evil spirits.

If a mother gives birth to two children who die in infancy, she will place a single blue bead in the left earlobe of her next child as a good luck charm. Some families will customarily cut off the top of a child's left ear instead; others give the child to its maternal grandmother to look after, as in the picture above, and not allow the head to be shaved until it has lost all its milk teeth.

RIGHT: A married woman wearing all the accessories associated with her tribe: brass lip plug, beaded collar decorated with bleached snail shells, leaf-like ear ornaments, and metal earrings from which hang tiny rings of goat horn.

The Turkana travel lightly. This herdsman (*right*) carries his wooden stool and a bow and arrow to protect his small stock from predators such as the golden jackal (*above*). I photographed this uncommon subspecies of the jackal family near the foothills of Mount Lapur, a striking feature rising 3000 feet above the surrounding plains, a short distance from the northwest corner of Lake Turkana.

2
Homestead Life

COMPARED WITH OTHER pastoralists of East Africa, such as the Maasai and Samburu, the Turkana live their lives in conspicuously unfavourable surroundings. They struggle for existence in a land where man pits his skills against nature by migrating constantly according to the needs of his stock. Although most families try to maintain a permanent base for their old people, and for animals with calves too young to travel, never a month passes without the stock camps moving in search of new pasture. In the dry season, when grazing and water are scarce, they often move every three days. Unencumbered by the trappings of modern living, donkeys assure the Turkana of complete mobility.

The construction of huts varies with the availability of materials, and the type of livestock the family owns. The stockless communities, or those possessing only a few goats, tend to build the most elaborate homes because they do not need to migrate. Some of the structures at Lodwar and the settlements close to Lake Turkana are beautifully made from bundles of doum palm fronds tied tightly together around a circular frame.

The truly nomadic communities build the most simple homes since there is little time to do more. No building materials are carried on the move. All will be collected afresh at each new camp, although materials from old, unoccupied homesteads nearby may be reused. In the dry season, the head of a large family may divide his home into two or three parts according to the differing requirements of his cattle, camels, sheep, and goats, but this will also depend on labour. No matter how many wives a man marries, each must build an *akai* (sleeping quarters) of her own. The senior wife will build hers on the right of the stock entrance, junior wives to the left.

Relations between the wives are generally very good. They all lend a hand with the thorn scrub stockpens, whose entrances must face east. They also cooperate over the daily chores and often help one another to build their rudimentary homes. A framework of pliable branches and saplings is interwoven and tied into a dome shape with strips of bark or *amooja* (wild sisal) fibre. They afford scant protection from the elements and no privacy, for one can see right through them. Nevertheless, they are probably the coolest type of dwelling that can be contrived given the materials available. They will be used by the wife and her children to sleep because her husband prefers his *etiam* (open sleeping enclosure) during dry weather; this is where she will visit him when summoned. Only in the rainy season will he deign to sleep in one of his wives' homes. Hides will be laid over the top of them and tied down with leather thongs to keep dry the food reserves and personal possessions that hang from the roof. His first wife keeps his ceremonial paraphernalia and branding iron in her home. Unmarried men and youths always sleep out in the open behind the stockpen for goats. Girls of a marriageable age will have a communal hut behind the cattle and camel pens with an entrance facing discreetly away from the main homestead.

Each wife will also build herself an *ekol* (day hut). These are made in much the same way as the sleeping quarters, but they will be somewhat taller, larger structures, and most likely have a light covering of branches as shelter from the punishing daytime heat. They are a hive of activity throughout the day. Women and their teenage daughters look after the young children, prepare skins, stitch leather, sew or fashion beads, and make wooden or leather containers. They display the tremendous ingenuity of people who flourish in adversity.

Due to their nomadic existence, the Turkana's artistic talent and expression are limited to personal clothing,

LEFT: The nomadic Turkana move their stock camps frequently in search of better pasture. In the dry season, when grazing and water are scarce, they might move every three days.

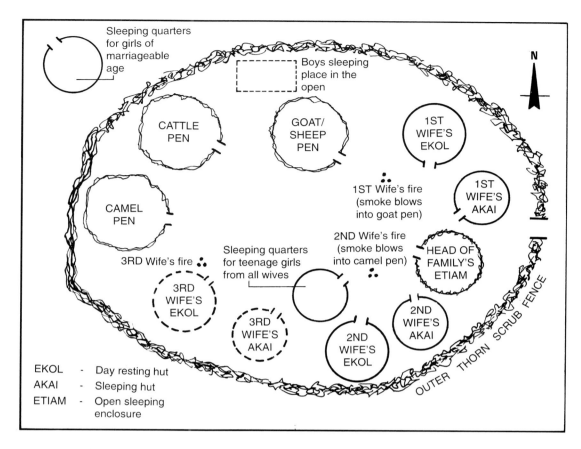

Sleeping quarters for girls of marriageable age

Boys sleeping place in the open

N

CATTLE PEN

GOAT/ SHEEP PEN

1ST WIFE'S EKOL

1ST Wife's fire (smoke blows into goat pen)

1ST WIFE'S AKAI

CAMEL PEN

2ND Wife's fire (smoke blows into camel pen)

HEAD OF FAMILY'S ETIAM

3RD Wife's fire

Sleeping quarters for teenage girls from all wives

3RD WIFE'S EKOL

3RD WIFE'S AKAI

2ND WIFE'S EKOL

2ND WIFE'S AKAI

OUTER THORN SCRUB FENCE

EKOL - Day resting hut
AKAI - Sleeping hut
ETIAM - Open sleeping enclosure

ornamentation, and household wares. Both men and women excel in wood and leather work. Gourds are scarce and expensive, and potters rare, because clay pots are impractical, breaking easily on the move. Consequently, trees are vital to their way of life which has led them to maintain a balance between conservation and exploitation.

A husband keeps away from his wives' day huts unless he falls sick, in which case he stays there to receive medication. When old, men laze and gossip with their age-mates under a shady tree not too far distant from the homestead. They talk for a while, sleep for a while and spend long hours playing *bau*, a game that is found in various forms all over Africa.

Senior elders head their households, fiercely independent family units which are affiliated to larger extended family groups through marriage and a carefully cultivated network of stock friends. Though the elders are auto-cratic by nature, everyone in the household, unlike the neighbouring tribes, has the right to an opinion, including women and children.

Except in the dry season, stockowners cannot move freely and graze wherever they please. Even use of the large, wet-season grazing areas is restricted to a number of specific families who usually share the same cattle brands. This encourages extended families to live together since they have a well developed sense of belonging. Territorial rights vary and depend on the proximity of riverine forests and woodlands. In these areas the tribe will have established a system of *ekwar* (ancestral user-rights) which give a family specific harvesting rights to dry season fodder. Such 'ownership' is fairly flexible but works efficiently. In Kaputir, where the Ng'ikebootok terri-torial section of hunter-gatherers live, the concept extends to termite mounds where 'flying ants' are harvested exclusively by known families.

In the past, tribal loyalty was so extreme that the elders strongly objected to outsiders learning too much about Turkanaland. They still have an intolerant suspicion of strangers bordering on unfriendliness which can be disconcerting. Sometimes, visitors to a homestead are so completely ignored, it almost seems they must be invis-ible. No civilities are offered or enquiries made as to what they might want. Only after a frosty silence might greetings be exchanged. This is probably because strangers do not understand Turkana etiquette. The head of the family will seldom talk to a visitor until all his animals have been penned for the night.

Once a newcomer overcomes this initial reticence, he will realize the Turkana are a happy people despite life being a never-ending struggle in a land devoid of luxuries. There is no room for conspicuous generosity, for there are rarely any surpluses. On the other hand, they are ungrudging to their close friends and relatives who are made welcome and offered a share of whatever might be available. If there is nothing, they will stay for at least a day without eating. People live by constant sharing and begging which can be irksome to foreigners who dislike being pestered. Wherever visitors go in Turkanaland, people of all ages attempt to relieve them of their possessions. This irritating practice is considered an art and a game. Everyone acts in his own self-interest to cajole and exact whatever takes his fancy though chewing tobacco will usually be demanded first. If a person is successful, he can build up his wealth. The secret is to know when to acquiesce and when to refuse. Since nothing is given freely in Turkana society, the maxim could well be 'that which you want, you must demand'. Indeed, there is no word in the Turkana language for 'thank you' because a favour must always be repaid even if it takes a generation or so to do so. The nearest word is *alakara* meaning 'I am glad'.

Decoctions of various herbs, roots, and bark are prescribed for most forms of sickness, although minor recurring ailments such as headaches and stomachaches may be treated by making incisions on a patient's forehead or abdomen and releasing 'bad blood' from the point of disorder. The Turkana remedy for noosebleeds is 'infallible'. During three successive nosebleeds, the sufferer's blood is collected in a receptacle and boiled dry. It is buried on each occasion at the left-hand side of the entrance to the family's goatpen. After the third nosebleed, two blue glass beads are threaded onto a single strand of hair from a giraffe's tail and worn by the person as a necklace. All at once, the affliction is cured.

Blue beads also feature in tooth extraction. The 'dentist' collects a pair of sturdy thorns from an *Acacia tortilis* tree and threads one blue bead onto each spike. Thick wire is then placed alongside the spikes and tied with the thin fibres of the wild sisal plant so that the wire and spikes are just a little wider than the offending tooth. The 'dentist' wiggles the tooth to and fro to loosen it while sliding the thorns and wire either side of it below the gum. At the right moment, he will grip his homemade 'forceps' purposefully and wrench out the tooth. His patient then faces east, cups his hands, and throws the tooth over his head. It will be retrieved by others and buried with the two blue beads on the west side of the homestead beneath a small shrub.

Hydatid disease is a common parasitic infection in domestic animals which leads to the growth of cysts. Camels are particularly prone to it and are the most infected herbivores the Turkana own. Whenever they are killed, which is rare, some of the offal and the cysts will be fed to pets which contract and spread the disease. Indeed, it is the dog which acts as host to the adult worm and transfers the ova to man. The first visible sign of the disease is the swelling of the abdomen due to the formation of large fluid-filled cysts; otherwise, a person may look quite healthy. The Turkana have the highest incidence of Hydatidosis in the world for a unique reason. A mother trains a dog to lick her infant clean after it vomits or defecates.

The Turkana have several traditional ways of dealing with the problem, some more effective than others. They range from herbal remedies and scarification, to drinking sheep's urine. Traditional surgery is also practised in a few remote areas though modern medicine can now cure the disease.

While traditional 'surgeons' and healers are widely respected in the community, they lack the following of successful diviners, *ng'imurok*, who also play a role in curing ailments and counteracting witchcraft. The best known belong to the Meturona cattle-brand division, whose supernatural powers date back two centuries. Legend recalls how Apatepes, a strange being — half ape, half man — lived with a pack of baboons until the Turkana caught him and brought him to Kakuma. There, he learnt how to speak and was transformed into a man. In time, he became famous for his occult powers and turned into a great and revered diviner. Lokerio was his most remarkable descendant, followed by two prominent men — Lokorijam and Kokoi.

According to legend, Lokorijam prophesied the coming of white men five years before the first European travellers reached Turkanaland. He called together all his warriors at the Kerio River and told them that strange people with white skins would come from a distant ocean of inestimable size with the intention of usurping power. In an attempt to keep them out, he ordered ten warriors to find a hornless billy goat with an unblemished white skin, take it to the shores of Lake Turkana, and club it to death. With its feet facing the lake, the young men had to slit open its belly and remove the intestines. Then, each grasping a handful of chyme (the partially digested stomach contents of the slaughtered animal), they had to scatter it along the lakeshore. Though Lokorijam gave specific instructions that no part of the animal should be eaten, half the young men could not resist. They cooked and ate a little fat before returning home. Lokorijam knew exactly what had happened and summoned his army so that everyone could hear first-hand what he had to say about this serious breach of discipline. After the five admitted their mistake, the diviner told them that now he was powerless to stop the ghost-like foreigners entering Turkanaland.

Years later, Kokoi predicted his own death. His nephew – a blind octogenarian living near Lodwar – related the story to me.

> My uncle woke one morning and summoned the whole family to tell us of his vivid dream. I must have been about eight years old at the time, and remember the day well. My uncle explained how four white men armed with rifles would come to look for him. Three would be riding donkeys, and one would be walking, leading his beast by a halter. My uncle told us that we should not be afraid or run away: none of us would be harmed. The white men's mission was to arrest him, helped by traitors from our tribe.
>
> My uncle went on to predict how he would be taken to a distant land and advised us to take good care of his livestock. 'You must continue to graze my animals at night as is my wont,' he ordered us. 'But if ever one is taken by a hyena, this will be a sure sign that I am dead.' He singled out three fine oxen and told us that if any of their humps turned red, it would reaffirm his death. He went on to explain how his wives and children should shave their heads, and his sons and brothers assemble to conduct the usual burial ceremony regardless of the whereabouts of his corpse.

Kokoi's uncanny predictions came true. In 1926, he was arrested and charged under the Witchcraft Ordinance and taken to Eldoret prison where, unaccustomed to the cold, damp climate, he fell ill and quickly died of pneumonia. His death took place about the time of an eclipse of the sun. This is viewed as a bad omen by stockowners who have to kill several goats and sprinkle chyme over the rest of the animals to prevent the spread of disease. On this occasion, the Turkana believed Akuj was bringing wrath on his own people for conniving over Kikoi's death. It is notable that 1927 was a year of severe drought.

One of today's best known soothsayers is Joseph Natuba, a charismatic and dignified old man who lives at Lokiriama. Somewhat surprisingly for his trade, he professes to be a Christian. Natuba foretells the future in a number of different ways. He dreams at night and communes in his sleep with Akuj who will tell him when it will rain; he examines the intestines of cattle and goats making predictions accordingly; he puts a little tobacco into the palm of his right hand and interprets events by the pattern he sees; and his 'throwing' sandals are made of buffalo hide.

He came to prominence after dreaming of enemy raids and making a series of consistently accurate predictions giving the Turkana tactical advantage in defence and counter-attacks. Women and children were moved in time, while men stayed to fight. Because of his helping hand, he asserts that cattle can safely graze the area. Prior to 1973, it was too dangerous for them.

Natuba claims that Akuj will tell him in his dreams when it will rain. For example, in 1979 there was an acute drought and the people and their livestock suffered terrible hardship. An Irish priest visited Lokiriama every Saturday to hold an open-air mass at which he always prayed for rain. On one occasion, he asked Natuba to talk to him in private about the problem which was causing many of the wells to run dry. Natuba accompanied him to the mission at Lorugumu, sixty miles distant, where his friend the priest predicted rain in four days time. Natuba said nothing. The fourth day came without any sign of rain. By the ninth day of clear blue skies, the priest became agitated and asked Natuba for his own predictions. Natuba told him to bring four goats, and he would let him know. He then sent for an old man living near the mission who was told to summon three other old men and bring with them a goat with an unblemished black skin. Natuba killed the goat and inspected its intestines before eating it with the others. On yet another cloudless morning, he called the priest over and told him that there would be very heavy rain that evening; and so it came to pass. The long dry spell broke with torrential rain lasting several hours. All the *luggas*, the seasonal rivers, flowed in torrents which prevented Natuba from returning home.

ABOVE AND RIGHT: Donkeys are indispensable beasts of burden, assuring the nomadic Turkana of complete mobility. These sturdy little animals carry the few essentials of life in oval panniers strapped to their flanks; these have a frame of wickerwork onto which are tied thin strips of twisted hide. Infants, puppies and new-born kids will also ride securely in them. A very old or sick person may sit astride an animal if he or she is unable to walk.

Women are entirely responsible for building their homes. The fronds of doum palms make an ideal building material for semi-permanent dwellings in places where there is no grass for thatch. They remain surprisingly cool during the heat of the day but the occupants often sleep outside at night. Huts of a similar style can be found at Lokiriama in the west of the district but as doum palm trees do not grow there, the large bayonnet-tipped leaves of the wild sisal plant, *sansevieria*, are used instead.

LEFT: A woman makes the final ties to the framework of her sleeping quarters. In wet weather, hides will be laid on top and tied down with leather thongs.

The Turkana living along the Kerio River build their houses on stilts. This innovative style is found nowhere else in the district but suits the conditions at Lokori where the friable soil becomes a quagmire in heavy rain. It has the added advantage of lessening the problem of termite infestation and increasing air circulation, thus reducing the risk of malaria in an area where the cerebral strain is endemic.

RIGHT: The young boy sitting on the platform of his raised home is wearing a strip of goatskin round his neck. A traditional healer will have ordered the entire family to wear these as a prevention or cure for illness, or to ward off evil spirits.

A woman cuts down tree branches which she will use to fence her family's stock pens.

LEFT: A Turkana homestead at Lokiriama in the far west of Lodwar District. Mount Moroto rises more than 10,000 feet in the distance. This impressive mountain, which is in Uganda, is the highest feature of the Uganda Escarpment. The Karamojong live nearby.

Almost everything a family owns is kept in a wife's day hut. Wooden containers and utensils, gourds, and personal clothing or ornaments hang from the roof and walls. Watering troughs, donkey panniers and a grinding stone are stored against the walls. The only activity which takes place outside the hut is cooking. A woman's daughter will look after the young children and make herself useful around the home.

RIGHT: When families form temporary stock camps in the dry season, they might have to move again after three or four days, if grazing and water are scarce. Often, there is no time or inclination to build a temporary home. They will make do with a shady tree and sleep on skins spread out on the ground.

54

ABOVE AND RIGHT (BELOW): The Turkana are the only people in Kenya who still make adornments from ostrich eggshells using crude tools. Archaeological evidence suggests that the practice was widespread thousands of years ago but gradually died out as the habitat of the largest flightless birds in the world diminished. Now the Turkana are having difficulty finding enough eggshells for the painstaking job of making the thousands of little round discs that are needed to adorn the traditional aprons and broad leather belts of the young girls.

ABOVE: Ostrich chicks hatch in a scoop in the ground. The adult birds take it in turns to sit on the clutch of fifteen to twenty eggs for the forty-two days it takes them to incubate. The chicks keep their speckled feathers until they are about eleven months old. Only one per cent will attain maturity; the rest will be preyed on by hyenas, jackals, vultures and a host of other small predators.

The most common dye is made from the flowers of *Caralluma russelliana* which are boiled in water. They produce a colour range from light brown to almost black depending on dilution; the liquid is used to dye leather too. The Turkana call the flower *ekabose* (the foul smelling carcass) for it has a vile smell akin to rotting flesh. The pulp of the fleshy stems when boiled with minimal water for several hours is an effective arrow poison.

RIGHT: The Turkana are skilled craftsmen. The people of Kalakol on the shores of Lake Turkana weave attractive baskets from the dried fronds of doum palm trees. Vegetable dyes are used to create the simple but effective decorative patterns.

The Turkana excel at wood and leatherwork. The variety and shapes of wooden vessels, bowls and utensils show impressive beauty and grace, and are often attractively decorated with a red-hot poker to mark individual ownership. Generally, they are made from *Ekware* (*Gardenia volkensii*), whose fruits are emetic and purgative, and *Ekuruchanait* (*Delonix elata*), which grows throughout the dry bush country. Water and milk containers are hewn from Commiphora trees. Green wood is carved and until properly seasoned, will be well oiled with animal fat to prevent the objects splitting.

RIGHT: Childhood is very brief in nomadic communities. From an early age, girls help their mothers with the household chores, while boys learn to look after small stock. There will be only short periods in a day for them to relax and play.

Once a girl reaches puberty, her mother will carve her a small fertility doll, *ikideet*, which will often show obvious signs of being pregnant. These dolls vary from the very basic to the elaborate, and all will be clothed and embellished with a selection of the girl's own beads and a small piece of leather cut from her cloak. Every evening, she takes her doll down from the very top of her mother's hut where it hangs during the day, and sleeps with it close to her chest. Occasionally she sings it lullabies or talks to it by name. At other times, she will clutch it standing beside her mother as they face a new moon, uttering a prayer for her to have as many children as possible when she grows up.

RIGHT: Young boys and girls at play.

LEFT AND ABOVE: A young boy draws his bow to aim at a ground squirrel. He gives his small kill to his younger brother, who decorates a tuft of hair on the crown of his head with its fluffy tail. The style in which a boy's hair is cut or shaved will depend on his father's cattle brand division within the tribe.

Two sisters milk their family's nanny goats at dawn. At a tender age, children are 'given' a nanny goat of their own, which they will learn to milk. They will always have first call of the milk.

LEFT: A proud father and his young daughter; their hairstyles are typical of Turkana custom in the west of the district.

Enclosures for new-born kids and lambs are built off the ground to allow air to circulate, and keep the animals cool during the stifling heat of day.

RIGHT: Young men catch hold of a steer to throw it to the ground. The Turkana have a thorough knowledge of animal anatomy, and the trees and plants suitable for veterinary use.

A Turkana trader with gourds, grown and decorated by the Dodoth of Uganda. Turkanaland is mostly too dry for the climbing plant to survive, yet gourds are popular water containers. A large one costs as much as a goat.

LEFT: In semidesert areas, the collection of firewood may involve walking great distances for a meagre armful of twigs. Like other Nilotic peoples, Turkana women balance heavy loads on their heads with graceful carriage and poise.

LEFT: Women work as men play: this group of women carries water gourds on their heads. Waterholes can be a considerable distance from their homesteads.

BELOW: *Bau* is a game played by men throughout Africa. The Turkana version, *ng'ikiles*, is more complicated than most. Instead of two rows of shallow holes carved out of a wooden board or scooped from the ground, there are four rows of between twelve and twenty-four holes each, depending on the number of would-be players. Two pebbles are placed in each hole and the players move them between the two rows nearest them in an anti-clockwise direction with the aim of accumulating as many of their opponents pebbles as possible. It is puzzling to make out how many players are on either side because everyone seems to give advice at the same time or help randomly with the moves!

ABOVE AND RIGHT: A little way from the homestead and invariably situated to the east – the direction from which come life, light and the sun – stands a tree where the men rest up during the day. In the relative cool of its shade the elders hold court and, in past years, judged murder cases, adultery or theft.

ABOVE LEFT: The Turkana suffer from the highest incidence of hydatid disease in the world. The first visible sign of the disease, which is passed to humans by dogs, is the swelling of the abdomen, like this young boy at Nachola in southeast Turkanaland.

ABOVE RIGHT AND RIGHT: The Turkana have a great fondness for dogs which suffer from the rigours of famine like everyone else. They have always been an integral and intimate part of Turkana life. Small, light brown in colour and very affectionate, they warn their masters of night-time intruders and prowling predators. Women own more dogs than men and are rarely seen without one at heel. They sleep in the small enclosed space of the family home and are specially trained to help care for infants who are susceptible to attack by wild animals.

The wrist knife and ivory rings of Joseph Natuba, a well-known soothsayer living at Lokiriama.

LEFT: In case of illness, a person may approach a traditional healer who will diagnose the cause of sickness in different ways. Often, he will tell his patient to bring a goat of a specific colour, size and sex and explain where to find it. The goat is killed and its intestines examined before the healer smears his patient with chyme — the partially digested stomach contents of the slaughtered animal — to signify the giving of strength and protection. If the person is married, his wife and children may be smeared too.

Logilani Losikiria is a diviner who lives in south Turkanaland. He foretells the future, and unravels the past, by 'throwing' a pair of traditional leather sandals and interpreting events by the pattern they form on the ground. These sandals must never be worn though he will use them as a pillow at night. He will only take them from his house to prophesy.

ABOVE, RIGHT AND BELOW: When he has clients (*above*), Logilani will sprinkle a little green tobacco and spit the masticated pulp of the tender roots of *ekeriau* (a small plant which is believed to act as a charm) over the sandals as a blessing (*right*). Then holding them in his right hand, toes forward and soles inwards, he knocks the sides on the ground before spitting on them a second time. Next (*below*), he throws them into the air with a flick of the wrist. He has an excellent reputation for his accurate predictions which have made him famous beyond the borders of his own tribe.

3

Ornamentation and Dress

TURKANA DRESS IS uniquely different from any other tribe in Kenya. Judging by the descriptions of the first travellers to the region, the styles and ornaments of men have changed quite significantly this century, but the attire of women and girls has not.

All adult men carry two typical accessories, a wooden stool for comfort and a wrist knife for security. Stool styles vary from area to area and seem to be partially influenced by the neighbouring tribes. Commonly rectangular in shape and hewn from a solid piece of hardwood, they have a gently curving concave seat supported by two straight legs or a slim central leg which is rounded at the base. In the latter style, the bottom of the base is scooped out to prevent it slipping on smooth ground, and the owner can use the indentation to grind his tobacco into snuff. The wrist knife is worn on the right wrist like a bracelet unless a man is left-handed. In former times, it was a lethal weapon for close combat fighting. While still used for personal protection, it is now much more a multipurpose sharp instrument, useful for skinning animals, cutting up meat, and a host of other functions for which others might use a penknife.

Men do not wear much in the way of personal ornaments. They make do with a string or two of beads round the neck and one round the waist. Glass beads have now replaced the elaborate necklaces Teleki saw which were made of six individual stout rings of brass, copper or iron wire set one on top of each other and curved so tightly round the neck that they restricted movement. Brass or copper found its way to Turkanaland from the elephant hunters of Abyssinia, while local iron was bought from the Labwor blacksmiths of Uganda. The rows of coloured plastic bangles worn round the upper arm today have replaced the traditional coiled metal armlets and thick ivory bracelets, which went out of fashion after the elephant herds were decimated at the turn of the century.

It was customary for the Turkana to have two distinctive facial ornaments. A neat hole was pierced in the flesh below a man's lower lip soon after his initiation. A flat circular plug was then positioned in the mouth with a spigot protruding through the hole. When the wound had healed, a round or oval-shaped ornament, made of ivory or white quartz, was affixed to the spigot. Men's ornaments were at one time as large as a billiard ball but have shrunk over the years to the more manageable size of a golf ball. Only one or two communities still wear them, though there are many middle-aged men with pierced holes below their lips.

The septum of a man's nose was also pierced to allow a flat brass or aluminium nose plate to hang down over the lower face. These peculiar ornaments are oval or leaf shaped, often with a thin ridge running vertically down the centre and roughly patterned with abstract designs. Sometimes large enough to cover the mouth and chin, and invariably used on all ceremonial occasions, they must have been exceedingly awkward to wear.

Over the years, men's nakedness has given way to thin, striped blankets knotted over one shoulder or lengths of plain or printed cotton material wrapped around the waist. In the old days, full leopard skins were worn down the back as brilliant cloaks on all ceremonial occasions. Every man would kill and skin his own, which shows how numerous these predators were in the rocky hills and mountains of the district. Today, this style of dress has all but disappeared as a result of strict game laws intended to halt the decline of the leopard population.

Tight fitting leggings made of soft, white calf skin were always worn below a man's calves as a reliable protection from the wicked thorns afflicting herdsmen and travellers on long journeys through the scrub. Though these are now out of fashion, many men have taken to wearing the top half of socks round their ankles, more for

LEFT: A fine clay hairstyle so typical of the Southern Turkana. The black ostrich feather pompoms indicate that the man belongs to the *ng'imor* (black) moiety of his tribe.

decorative purposes than any meaningful form of protection. Others may wear small metal chains, two rows of cowry shells backed onto leather, or even thin strips of skin from a wild animal. Variations are numerous.

People who disregard clothes generally pay great attention to their hair. The most distinctive feature of a Turkana man's attire is his finely decorated clay hairdo. Styles have varied considerably since the days of the sack-like creation described by nineteenth-century travellers. The sack was long and flat, and hung down a man's back, below his shoulder blades. It increased in length as the wearer grew older and braided the hair of his dead relatives into his own. The hair was coated with grey clay and had an opening on the inner side in which he kept oddments such as snuff and his firesticks. Often a hoop, made of fine segmented bones bound with giraffe hair, was inserted and curved over the head of the wearer with a black ostrich feather pom-pom on the end. These hairstyles belonged to the age when men wore iron rings as necklaces and iron-studded leather belts. In the 1920s and 1930s, the style changed to one similar to today's except that the buns were decorated with the thin curved stalks of dried calabashes.

The present fashion is small and neat, and has to be reworked every three or four months. A man's hair is divided by a transverse parting from ear to ear. Hair on the front of the head is short, but the back is usually long. The hairdresser sets to work first on his client's hair at the back of the crown. He coats it with glutinous grey clay. Once it has been layered, plastered, and shaped into an elliptical bun, he will tie several ostrich feather holders into it. The single holders are made from dried cows' teats. However, if more substantial multifeather holders are preferred, the pounded sinews of oxen will be interwoven with thin strands of copper wire to form oblong or square blocks standing about one centimetre high. Perforated with numerous small holes, they are suitable for lavish displays. Before the clay sets, it may be coloured with the powder of a pulverized blue rock and stippled by a special wooden comb. Nowadays Colman's azure blue, a proprietary clothes whitener, is widely used by tribesmen living east of Lake Turkana. Mr Reckitt and Mr Colman would be amazed at the range of uses found for their product!

The hairdresser then works on the front part of the head. This is where styles vary quite considerably. Those living in the west of the district prefer a plain fawn or buff coloured finish, which is somewhat thinner and broader than the fashions further east. There, the frontpiece is an orange coloured strip about an inch wide, but if the wearer is middle-aged, he may want to feature a small oval design in the centre; these will be neatly decorated with whatever natural pigments are found in the area. While the thin strip is usually stippled, the larger style is plain.

As a final touch to these elaborate coiffures, elders may opt to have the chosen colours of their particular age-grade and territorial section carefully painted round the edge of the bun. The creation is then ready to be embellished with a startling array of fine ostrich feathers. A billy goat can be bartered for one or two of the finest white feathers, but this number may increase to ten if they are short and of mediocre quality. The Somali or blue-neck ostrich is indigenous to the northern districts of Kenya and male birds have finer, white tail and wing feathers than the Maasai or red-neck ostrich to the south. Feathers are not simply a matter of personal preference. The colour a man will wear is entirely dependent on his moiety. The *ng'irisae* wear pure white or dyed russet-red feathers from female ostriches whereas the *ng'imor* wear off-white, brown, grey or black feathers from male ostriches. By tradition, the finest white feathers from male ostriches were only worn by very old men of the *ng'imor* moiety and their wives, but everyone covets them these days.

Women and girls have a great love of beads of all shapes and sizes. Coloured glass beads from the Czech Republic (glass beads from Central Europe first came to Africa in 1560 and were used to trade); black seeds, *emus*, from wild banana plants growing close to the lake; small brown seeds, *edome*, from the edible fruits of *Cordia sinensis*; two or three rows of cowry shells stitched onto leather; ostrich shell beads; iron beads; and *ekeriau*, beads made from a strong smelling root which are believed to act as a charm and protect the wearer from man or beast. Whatever combination a woman chooses to wear, they all glisten with animal fat. Animal fat, plain or mixed with red ochre or charcoal dust, is also applied to the upper part of their bodies to keep their skin soft.

Sometimes, pendants are added to necklaces; one of the most popular is cut and shaped from the large, white snail shells that are found in the arid north.

The numerous necklaces worn by teenage girls will be given to them by their parents and elder brothers, never a boyfriend. A married woman will only remove her necklaces if she is taken seriously ill or for three days after her husband's death. Otherwise, they are worn night and day throughout her life. It is a symbol of real wealth when a woman can comfortably rest her chin on her *ng'akoromwa* (broad-beaded collar) which is shown off on top of her strings of beads. As long as her bride wealth has been paid, a married woman must also wear a plain metal ring around her neck. Called *alagama*, it is the Turkana equivalent of a wedding ring. If the woman is married to a man of the *ng'irisae* moiety, she will wear one made of yellow metal such as brass or copper, if to a man of the *ng'imor* moiety, black or white metal such as iron or aluminium.

While men and boys are indifferent to clothes, women and girls have always taken a keen interest in dressing stylishly. Hardly a week goes by that they do not make a new article of clothing from tanned sheep or goatskins which are expertly colour-matched and sewn. Unmarried girls wear two V-shaped aprons made of tanned goatskins with the hair removed — a small one in front and a larger one behind. The front apron is decorated round the edge of the V with a broad band of ostrich eggshell beads. These are pierced and strung together before being sewn onto the garment. In places where ostrich eggshells are no longer obtainable, the shape of the front apron is generally rectangular, and coloured glass beads are used instead. In the far west of the district, aprons may be made from strips of plaited leather. However, the plaited fibres of the wild sisal plant often replace leather. It is almost impossible to tell the difference between the two except that the fibres are a lighter colour, and the aprons are somewhat longer, reaching below the knee. Irrespective of the differing styles of a girl's front apron, the V- shaped rear aprons are invariably plain and just long enough to touch the ground. They are held in place with a broad leather belt, embellished with ostrich eggshell beads, cowry shells, or brightly coloured glass beads.

Girls complete their wardrobe of practical, home-made clothes with full-length cloaks of soft skin, which are richly decorated. They hang loosely down the front of the body but may be tied round the waist if the girl is journeying far. Married women also wear leather cloaks but theirs are plain.

The aprons of married women are never decorated with ostrich eggshell beads. The front apron is made of calf, goat, sheep, or gazelle skin without the hair removed. Though fashion and family tradition dictate the style and length, it is usually short of the knee and trimmed with home-made metal beads to keep it in place. Several lines of iron, copper or brass beads may also be sewn in the centre of the apron in preference to glass beads. A long time ago when metal was scarce, small soft stone beads were used instead. The full length back skirt swishes noisily along the ground and is made of hairy goatskins. Styles differ from territorial section to section. Some women stitch dark and light skins in successive broad vertical bands. Others sew alternate black and brown squares. A number of cattle brand divisions require their women to edge the lower sides of their skirts with the front leg skins of their marriage oxen.

Belt styles also vary. A few are decorated with metal beads, others with cowry shells, and still others are made with the metacarpus and metatarsal bones of dikdiks, one of the smallest and daintiest of Kenya's antelopes. Two bones are found in each foot, so an average size belt means the death of about seven dikdiks.

Lip ornaments worn by married women differ quite considerably from those of men. Like their menfolk, however, they pierce the outer rim of their ears four to eight times, depending on family tradition. Tiny circular pieces of goat horn and an occasional glass bead are attached to small brass rings and worn through the holes. Some women now prefer to wear metal pendants made from old aluminium cooking pots. The pendants are oval or leaf shaped, somewhat similar in style and pattern to a man's nose plate, but less than a quarter of the size. They tend to accentuate a person's ears because the sides of the head are shaved and the ridge of hair remaining on top is braided into numerous small plaits which fall untidily over the crown.

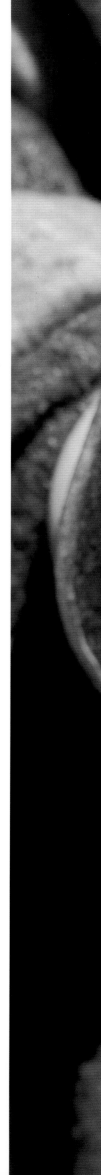

ABOVE AND RIGHT: Turkana men never leave home without a small wooden stool which doubles as a pillow to protect their elaborate hairdos from being damaged during sleep. Everyone carves his own – a light, easy-to-carry, all-purpose affair made from a solid piece of hardwood. Some men take great pains to decorate theirs with caricatures of wild animals and birds while others set store by the quality of leatherwork on the legs and carrying handles.

Wrist knives are also worn by adult men. The razor-sharp round blades of beaten iron are about two inches wide and, when not in use, are sheathed in leather. Originally a weapon for personal protection and close-combat fighting, they double up as an all-purpose knife.

ABOVE AND RIGHT: Elders with decorative ivory lip ornaments. These are secured in position by a spigot inserted in a hole which is pierced below the lower lip after a man's initiation. This singular form of decoration was once widespread in the region but is gradually dying out.

FOLLOWING PAGE, LEFT: An old man wears a nose plate made from discarded aluminium cooking pots. It is hooked through a hole in the median septum of his nose. Before the introduction of aluminium, nose plates were made of brass which was traded for ivory by elephant hunters from Abyssinia (now Ethiopia).

FOLLOWING PAGE, RIGHT: Black ostrich feathers decorate the front part of this man's traditional clay hairstyle. Small metal chains, with or without beads attached to the ends of them, have become commonplace as ear ornmaments. They have replaced the old style when men hung small brass or iron rings from four to eight holes pierced in the outer rim of each ear.

ABOVE AND LEFT: Every Turkana elder used to wear a leopard skin cape on all ceremonial occasions which just went to prove the large number of these predators in the district. The strict enforcement of game laws and the depredations of poachers to satisfy the past dictates of high society fashion have resulted in this traditional style of dress rapidly disappearing. Also on ceremonial occasions, elderly men, especially those who are balding, prefer to wear removable headgear. One of the most fashionable styles is a close fitting skullcap with a design in front representing the small clay portion of the traditional hairstyle. The back 'bun' is made from the moulded breast capes of white or pink-backed pelicans which are trapped along the shores of Lake Turkana.

ABOVE: An expert hairstylist smears clay on the crown of a man's head, then fashions it into the distinctive elliptical bun which is so charactersitic of the Turkana.

LEFT: Before the clay bun hardens, the hairdresser will insert into it ostrich feather holders and smooth the clay once more. The holders are made of dried cows' teats.

RIGHT: A finely decorated clay hairstyle. The markings round the edge of the bun denote the man's age grade and territorial section within the tribe.

The blue-neck, or Somali ostrich, is found in northern Kenya. It has finer plumage than the red-neck, or Maasai, ostrich common in the south of the country. The photograph shows a male displaying during the mating season.

RIGHT: The magnificent white ostrich feathers worn in the clay hairstyle of this elder are from a blue-neck ostrich. The colour of feathers a man wears depends on his moiety of which the Turkana have two. The feathers are kept in a wooden tube when not in use.

ABOVE: Years ago, iron and brass bracelets were common, but are seldom seen these days.

RIGHT: The ostrich feather holders affixed to the top of this man's clay hairstyle are made from the pounded sinews of an ox intertwined with thin brass wire. The holders are ideal for multifeather displays. Note the round quid of chewing tobacco behind the man's left ear.

FAR RIGHT: A man sporting an impressive array of feathers. Having shunned the discomfort of an ivory lip ornament, he has to wear a small wooden plug in the hole pierced below his lower lip to prevent dribbling.

ABOVE AND RIGHT: The ornaments that women insert in a hole pierced below their lower lips are varied and differ in style from those of their menfolk. Some are gently curving and beautifully made from twisted and braided strands of copper and brass wire with a large red bead hanging on the end; a tight fitting aluminium ball attached to the other end acts as a plug to secure the ornament in the mouth. Some equally attractive styles are made solely of copper wire and have no bead; others are wood, cylindrical in shape like a short round rod; and yet others are fashioned from ivory but retain the cylindrical shape. Bleached shells of the African land snail are a popular adornment to necklaces.

FAR LEFT: The number of necklaces a woman wears reflects her husband's wealth. If she marries into a rich family, she is given so many strings of beads that her chin will rest comfortably on her *ng'akoromwa* (beaded collar) without her lowering her head. Brass ear ornaments are rarely seen and also indicate wealth.

ABOVE: A woman wears an ivory lip ornament and necklaces of green beads, a colour associated with lush grass and worn solely for beauty.

LEFT: An old woman in a remote area of Turkanaland wears attractive home-made necklaces. The strings are made up of the irregular black seeds of the wild banana plant, small brown seeds of the *Diospyros scabra* tree, and paler seeds from shrubs of the *Grewia* genus. Coloured glass beads were introduced to the Turkana by Abyssinian elephant hunters more than a century ago. One of the first to be traded was a large blue bead of Dutch manufacture, called *lokwango*, which is rarely seen today.

ABOVE, LEFT AND FOLLOWING PAGES: There is much that can be learnt from the language of beads because every colour has a meaning and reason for being worn. Red is the colour of blood, which wards off evil spirits that may haunt a person when someone dies. Blue is the colour of the sky, a sign of munifence, fertility, and an abundance of the necessities of a pastoral life. Black is the colour of shade and coolness, which is believed to keep sorcerers at bay and render curses harmless. Infants wear black beads round their necks, wrists or ankles as a prevention against illness. White is the colour of sacrificial animals used to ratify peace treaties, a sign of good things to come. Orange is the colour of dust devils which are propelled by the evil spirits of the dead bent on destruction. People wear this colour to commune with, and appease, their ancestors and to seek Akuj's help protecting their children. When a warrior chooses to wear orange, he is protected against injuries that may be sustained in a raid. Green is the colour of lush grass and chyme, and is worn solely for beauty.

Girls' necklaces are well-oiled with animal fat and glisten in the sun. Occasionally, a girl will put on so many that her vertebrae stretch and her neck muscles gradually weaken. The girl (*above*) has had the front of her head shaved to denote that her husband or father died recently. The natural gaps in her front teeth are considered a sign of great beauty.

Surrounded by her friends, a young girl scrapes the hair from a goatskin. After treatment and working it by hand, she will sew it into a personal garment adorned with brightly coloured glass beads.

RIGHT: Women are adept at preparing animal skins. Once a skin has been pegged out and sun-dried, all the little pieces of dried flesh and flaked skin are scraped off the back. Then, the powdered seeds of the poisonous white trumpet flower, *Datura stramonium*, are mixed with a little water to the consistency of thick porridge, rubbed into the skin to soften it and left for seven days. Finally, the skin is worked by hand for several more days until it is supple.

Scarification is practised by both men and women using a sharp home-made knife and the barb of an acacia tree. The Turkana do not practise circumcision so scarification is a way in which people can prove their capacity to withstand pain. While it is very much a matter of personal preference, women usually confine their decorations to their upper arms and abdomen. Men, on the other hand, may cover much of their torsos.

LEFT: A young married woman braids the hair of her friend. The hair is first worked with wood ash to straighten it. This makes it easier to style into small plaits. Her black leather apron is decorated with the front leg skins of her marriage ox, which is customary among several cattle brand divisions of the tribe.

Young girls return home from a waterhole. Their large containers are made of wood. The leather carrying straps are often embellished with glass beads, or cowry shells from the Indian Ocean. These shells are found in tribal decoration throughout Africa, having once been a medium of exchange.

RIGHT: When a girl's leather cloak becomes old and torn, she may sew circular patterns of beads on the usable parts. These are then cut out, strung together, and hung from her neck down the front of her body as an original and eye-catching decoration.

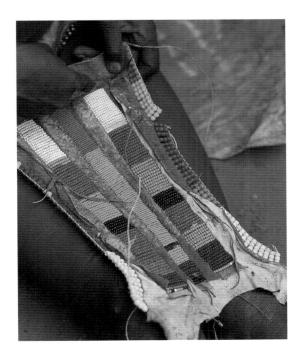
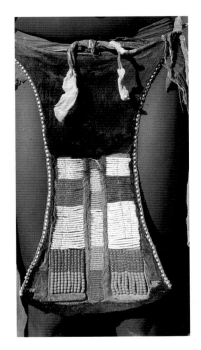

The leather aprons worn by women and girls are beautifully made and decorated. Married women edge theirs with home-made iron beads, and leave the skin hairy (*top right*). Girls must remove all the hair. Their V-shaped aprons are edged with ostrich eggshell beads (*bottom*), or are rectangular and decorated all over with coloured glass beads (*left and top left*).

A dikdik, one of Kenya's daintiest antelopes, which mates for life.

BELOW: Women make belts from the metacarpus and metatarsal bones of dikdiks. Two bones are found in each foot. Nowadays, many belts follow a similar pattern but are made of wood, like those on the opposite page.

RIGHT: The leather cloaks worn by unmarried girls are embellished with attractive beadwork.

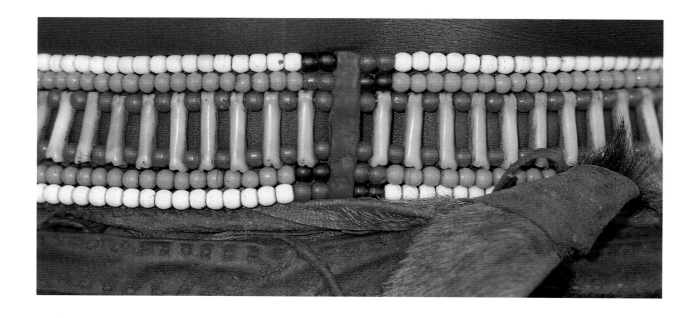

4

Pastoralism and Conflict

DESPITE UNRELIABLE RAINFALL and a dearth of good pasture, cattle are coveted by the Turkana. Though seldom slaughtered for meat, they will routinely provide a man's family with milk and blood besides being a useful source of clothing, footwear, bedding and shelter. No matter how many camels or flocks of sheep and goats a man owns, he will never count himself rich unless he owns cattle. They are the essence of his existence, a symbol of his standing in society, and the means which will allow him to marry as many wives as he desires. Without cattle, he cannot participate in important tribal ceremonies or join others at dances to sing in praise of his dance ox.

Every man from initiation until his death will have an *emong'* (dance ox) of his own. He chooses an ox for this purpose with a heavy bone structure, one with potential to grow into a magnificent bull. Colour is a matter of personal choice. A man will not necessarily confine his selection to his own herds. If he has no animal which appeals to him, he may seek one from his relatives or in-laws, but the process of begging it from them can be very tedious and drawn out. He will name the animal after one of its quirks and his friends will call him by the same name. When charging into battle, he will gain courage by shouting the name at the top of his lungs.

Whereas dance oxen are usually the finest animals a family owns and may have their horns manipulated or hides branded to distinguish them from others, they are not worshipped or treated much differently from the rest of the herd. They will even be slaughtered and eaten when they pass their prime since an owner may suffer misfortune if his dance ox dies of old age. If perchance it did, the meat could only be eaten by women, and no man would willingly allow that! As soon as one dance ox dies, another must replace it. If misfortune strikes and a dance ox is stolen, the owner will use every means possible to recapture it or avenge the theft by killing those responsible. Inaction would be a sign of cowardice and a stigma on the man for the rest of his life.

The Turkana are inordinately fond of singing and dancing. The song of the bulls, *edong'a*, is enjoyed by both sexes of all ages and invariably ends a dance session called the *akimumwar*. This often includes the suggestive mimicking of mating animals. The dancers form a circle, men on one side and girls on the other. Rhythm to the melodious singing is maintained by hand clapping and foot-stomping. Musical instruments are rare except for metal bells strapped to the dancers' legs. Each man takes centre stage in turn to sing the praises of his favourite beast.

If he does not own cattle, a man will sing the praises of his finest billy goat, which may have its horns manipulated in the same way as oxen. Only the stockless people living on the fringe of society are unable to perform the song of the bulls. The Ng'ikebootok hunter-gatherers end their *akimumwar* by singing in praise of bees, beehives, and the fruits of the forest, such as pumpkins and water melons. Likewise, the Ng'ibochoros, who are fishermen, sing about the doum palm trees, *Hyphaene thebaica*, to which they have user-rights and Lake Turkana, but interestingly never about fish.

Stockowners know each of their animals by name and notice immediately if one is missing — not by laboriously counting the herd but through their ability to picture instantly every animal in their mind. There are more than twenty words to describe the shape of horns and dozens more to denote the precise colours and markings

LEFT: Goats forage for browse in the semidesert terrain of Central Turkanaland. It rarely rains there, but a heavy downpour can cause severe soil erosion.

of every imaginable type of skin. All cattle have to be branded with the owner's family markings, one for male and another for female progeny. An animal's ears must also be cut in a special way to denote the man's moiety.

The herds give prestige and pride to his wives. Each is allocated a few milking cows to feed herself and her children; in the dry weather, only children will be given milk. At an early age, children with also be 'given' their own cow or nanny goat to milk. They usually drink fresh milk but adults often prefer to keep theirs in gourds suspended from a hut's rafters until it curdles. The senior wife will have the largest number of cattle since she must entertain her husband's guests. Mothers give their sons animals to start up their own herds. While a father may do the same when a son marries, his gift must eventually be repaid. Moreover, the animals will be grazed as part of his own herd until he dies whereupon the eldest son takes them over.

The onset of rain brings relief and happiness to herdsmen who drive their cattle down from temporary stock camps in the mountains to join their relatives on the plains. Animals put on condition surprisingly quickly; rib cages and hip bones disappear, and the cows lactate once more. July — *Losuban* (the month of plenty) in the Turkana calendar — is when most marriages take place. Social activity reaches a climax, and spontaneous dances are a nightly occurrence. But respite from the elements is short-lived. As the grass begins to wither, the stock is moved because grazing is never equally suitable for cattle, camels, sheep, and goats. Families split up and are unlikely to live together again for eleven months or more.

The splitting of families is a way of life peculiar to nomads and makes the people very self-reliant. Children from an early age are encouraged to act independently. Each must pull his or her weight in a nomadic society. As soon as they are old enough, children run errands and make themselves useful around the home. At about the age of four, a boy begins to look after his family's stock guided by an elder brother or close relative who constantly encourages him to think and act on his own until he is competent to handle any situation.

As girls grow up, they undertake household chores under the supervision of their mothers. By the age of ten, they are quite indispensable, routinely fetching and carrying water, collecting firewood, cooking and looking after their younger brothers and sisters. At the same time, they learn how to make leather garments, and wooden utensils or containers. This prepares them for marriage about the age of seventeen when they are fully matured. Their brothers of the same age are still uninitiated juveniles and have no real status in the tribe.

The head of a household makes all the decisions regarding his family's livestock. He stipulates where the herds should be grazed and which animals should be watered and when. Though Turkanaland is one of the driest places in East Africa, it is blessed with a reasonably high underground water table thanks to the surrounding mountains. This allows sweet water wells to be dug in most areas. Only at the height of a very dry season do water levels recede, requiring some wells to be dug to a depth of twenty-five to thirty-five feet. When the rains break a rush of water fills them with sand, so once or sometimes twice a year they have to be dug anew. Men and youths are responsible for this work.

It is lack of good pasture rather than water that forces the Turkana to trek great distances with their cattle, sometimes going two clear days without water. Animals are more likely to succumb through weakness from poor grazing than to disease because the district is surprisingly clear of stock diseases though rinderpest, anthrax and bovine pleuropneumonia do occur at times. Besides, the Turkana's knowledge of anatomy, and trees and plants suitable for veterinary use, is extremely thorough.

If the rains fail, large sections of the community teeter on the brink of catastrophe. Famine forces them to live for a while on wild fruits, berries, roots, and nuts which are also a useful supplement in times of plenty. There are no less than thirty types of edible berries that can be gathered by women at the right time of year. While some are eaten raw, others are boiled in water for several hours to reduce their extreme bitterness. Yet others are boiled, crushed, and then dried for emergency rations when food is scarce. Doum palm nuts are also dried, pounded, mixed with blood and dried again before being stored in skin bags. This intimate knowledge of the district's flora helps everyone to endure hard times.

The Turkana must follow the rain if their livestock is to survive. If they stay in one place until the grazing and water are finished, they will all perish. It is a complex process wresting the most from their environment. The elders try to predict where the rain will fall and be there just as the bare earth is covered with the first flush of succulent new grass. They sift through a mass of information gleaned from travellers passing through their neighbourhood. Moreover, they observe gathering rain clouds in far off places and keep a careful watch for lightning, judging the distance by plunging a polished spear upright into the ground. They sit facing the spear with their backs to the lightning and watch how far the lightning's reflection reaches down the blade and metal shaft. Years of experience tell them approximately how many days journey away the rain is falling: the shorter the reflection on the spear, the greater the distance away. The clear, cloudless nights of northern Kenya reveal a vast assemblage of stars. Most elders have a sound knowledge of the solar system for in a certain position one star will bring rain, another drought, another disease, and so on. Likewise, the moon is a reliable indicator of the weather. Also, the purposeful departure of flocks of white cattle egrets is a most certain sign of rain in the direction the birds fly.

The Turkana do not keep livestock merely because it has a bearing on the stark economics of staying alive. They have to grapple with a whole host of fundamental cultural and emotional issues which override the obvious advantages or disadvantages of tending different types of animals in semidesert terrain. However, if these issues are disregarded, it can be argued that camels and goats are much more important to the Turkana than cattle. Being browsers, they maintain condition in areas where cattle could not survive a single week. Goats reproduce two or three times a year and are a vital source of food. Goats' milk is considered particularly suitable for infants because the richer camels' milk with its high calcium content can cause indigestion. Even donkeys' milk will be consumed by children and adults who are too poor to enjoy any other type of milk. Goatskins are turned into women's clothes while surplus animals are sold to buy food, such as flour, tea, and sugar. It is true that goats can be destructive and ravage seedlings – there are those who term them the 'scourge of Africa' – but the flocks hardly ever reach the carrying capacity of the land before drought and disease cull them. As a result, overstocking is rare. If it does occur, it is generally too short for any long-term environmental degradation.

In an aerial census undertaken in 1990, it was estimated that the Turkana owned 415,000 head of cattle, 117,000 camels and 2.9 million sheep and goats. Since Turkana herdsman graze their stock in neighbouring countries from time to time, and their neighbours vice versa, I would treat these figures with circumspection. Besides, climatic conditions can alter figures dramatically from one year to the next.

The tribe has owned camels for upwards of 150 years. In spite of an Old Testament style legend of a diviner parting the waters of Lake Turkana for a raid that brought them camels from the east, it is generally recognized that they were acquired from the Boran and Rendille, who are camel owning nomads of Cushitic origin. Unlike the Cushites, the Turkana have never trained the camel as a pack animal.

Many families have been impoverished by disasters and subsist on their small stock and a camel or two. Other wretched people with no stock are excluded from the mainstream of their culture and society. However unfortunate the circumstances of their losses, stock owners are contemptuous of anyone who has suffered a complete stock wipe-out. They argue that wise men painstakingly build up a network of stock friends with whom they farm out or exchange animals to insure against natural disasters and stock raids. Based on convenience and mutual trust, it is the only stock tie a person may have that is not linked to kinship. While the obligation is reciprocal, it can be broken at any time.

Stock wipe-outs are not new in Turkanaland, but the means to redress them have changed. Cattle rustling and banditry are age-old pursuits in the region. Though forcibly curtailed in the 1920s, these vices never entirely died out because they are an important facet to the social and economic structure of tribal life. The problem dogged the colonial government and continues to trouble independent Kenya. Despite heavy prison sentences meted out to offenders, there will always be some members of society who are prepared to take the risk. Young braves raid for the sheer excitement of a fight or to enhance their standing in the community. Others, possibly poor but contemplating marriage, steal cattle in order to pay the bride wealth. A majority will join a raiding party out of the dire necessity to replenish or replace their herds and stave off the spectre of starvation. Today, these people find it almost impossible to correct their circumstances at someone else's expense. Gone are the carefree days of Turkana supremacy in all aspects of traditional warfare. Their long-time enemies now delight in exacting retribution. Access to modern automatic weapons in neighbouring countries wracked by civil strife, has been crucial to their success.

Victorious raids and acts of heroism still occupy the minds of many old people. Diviners such as Lokorijam and Kokoi, and the outstanding war leader, Ebei, stir people's emotions and prompt elders to relate melodramatic and exaggerated tales of their feats. No other people in Kenya talk so much on the subject of war. It is ingrained in them; they are constantly on their guard; and the continuing hostilities along the Ugandan, Sudanese, and Ethiopian borders keep the topic very much alive.

Until the advent of modern weapons, men used to carry two eight-foot-long spears with small narrow blades, a fighting stick, and a narrow rectangular shield made of giraffe or buffalo hide. For close quarter fighting, they wore a circular wrist knife and one or two finger knives on the forefingers of their left hands. These vicious little instruments of war were designed to gouge out an enemy's eyes. Earlier this century, the British colonial administration banned them from being made or worn because they were so dangerous.

The position of war leader was never an official appointment. Instead, a handful of men who had outstanding ability, personality and courage came to be recognized as such by their fellow tribesmen. The more successful they were, the greater became their personal following. War leaders called men to arms and sought the blessing of a local diviner before starting out on a raid. Participation was generally confined to anyone who had been initiated. The result was that men up to the age of fifty joined in so long as they were fit enough to withstand the pace. Youths were occasionally taken along as drovers but were expressly forbidden to enter the fray. More often than not, though, it was impossible to keep them out of trouble because they had been brought up with a strong will of their own and never took 'no' for an answer.

Feasting and dancing invariably preceded raids with the *akinyak* (male age-set dance) being performed repeatedly as women and girls taunted the participants into a frenzy by obscene posturing. The men divided themselves into their moieties and never merged into a single dance group. After scouts returned from detailed reconnaissance of the enemy and the disposition of their herds, the men would line up, facing east, while the diviner harangued them with last minute instructions from Akuj.

He then conducted a special purification ceremony to allay people's fears, and assure them of strength and invincibility. On occasions, he would summon a very old woman from the neighbourhood and order her to wash her breasts in a wooden stock trough filled with water. This water was then sprinkled over the combatants as they filed out of camp. At other times, he would make the men step over a large stone which he had buried and slept on at night, or crawl through an arch of thorns, in the belief that this would make the enemy slow to wake upon the morning of the raid. There was also a time when Kokoi told his followers that they would find a large African rock python, *akipom*, on the path they had to follow. Before jumping over it, he instructed them to stroke it gently four times, rubbing their foreheads and chests after each touch. He asserted this omen would portend a highly successful raid. Whatever form the ceremony took, the diviner ended up by smearing the men's naked fronts from head to foot with white clay.

The sight of a large party setting out on a raid must have been spectacular. Like armies of old, the best fighting troops went into battle properly dressed. Every man's clay bun was freshly plastered and decorated with his finest ostrich feathers. The war leader was distinguished from the rest by a magnificent tassel of six giraffe tails hanging from a leather thong secured just above his left elbow. His soldiers were a fine body of men all eager for a fight. Most standing six feet tall, they were at the very peak of physical fitness, with muscles rippling and not an ounce of fat on their bodies. They travelled quickly over long distances and lived frugally off the land.

Raids invariably took place at first light after a last furtive check on the enemy. Most tribes living on top of the Uganda Escarpment were sitting targets because agriculture had made them much less nomadic than the Turkana. Guile and stealth were the keys to success. The raiders would silently creep up on their enemy. At a given signal, they rushed from all directions shouting their ox names as they ran. While one group rounded up the cattle and drove them quickly out of the thorn scrub stock enclosures, the rest engaged their opponents ferociously in hand to hand fighting. Women and children were not spared, though young boys and girls were often taken prisoner and fully integrated into the families of their captors.

With victory assured, the raiders split into small groups and went in different directions to a prearranged rendezvous where they met after a day or so. The Turkana had a tactical advantage in this phase of any action because their low-lying geographical location enabled them to drive the rustled stock downhill for a quick getaway. The spoils were divided at the meeting place with the diviner's and war leader's generous shares being put aside first. A fight was not unusual for the rest because there was no concept of either equal shares or a split based on personal merit in the raid. Every man rushed to cut his cattle brand on as many animals as possible. Once properly marked, they became his property but there were many tussles, some violent, as men tried to prevent others from marking animals they had tentatively earmarked as their own. It seems an astonishing way to end a successful raid but anthropologists and psychologists express no such surprise. They feel that it perfectly fits the character of the people who are constantly having to create and defend their own interests.

The men who returned home with many cattle, had to pass on a share of the booty in the inevitable begging and redistribution routine to their fathers, brothers, uncles, cousins, in-laws and best friends. If that meant a raider had little left to show for his dangerous exploits, at least he had laid the foundation of a number of stock obligations on which he would unhesitatingly call in years to come. Before any demands could be made, however, he had to stop a short distance to the east of his father's homestead while his mother blessed him by sprinkling water over him and his spoils. His father and local elders then led him to a nearby thicket for a cleansing ceremony.

A pure black nanny goat was killed by slitting its stomach open and chyme mixed with blood poured over him. Next, the animal was roasted whole, and eaten. If he had killed an enemy during the raid and there was a witness to the feat, the front and sides of his hair were shaved leaving a small round patch on the back of his crown. This was fashioned into a clay hairstyle similar to the one that had been created for him during his initiation, except it was smothered in red ochre. The following day, he underwent scarification as a permanent manifestation of his courage. A day or so after the painful ordeal, he joined others dancing and feasting to celebrate victory.

LEFT: Red and yellow barbets build their nests in termite mounds. The Turkana consider that the loud and unmistakable bird call insults women, who throw hot ashes toward the birds if they sight them near the homestead.

BELOW: In all the miles of rich pasture between Kapedo and Lokori, not a single head of livestock can be seen. Fear of attack by the Pokot has delivered the land to wilderness.

RIGHT: Dotting the landscape near Lorionetom in northern Turkanaland are the tall ventilating flues of termite mounds, up to two or three times the height of a man. As a general rule, the higher the ambient temperature, the taller the flues. Their colour is often markedly different to the surrounding earth because the million-strong colonies of little insects that build these remarkable towers excavate soil in their fortressed galleries and tunnels from strata deep underground.

LEFT, ABOVE AND RIGHT: When a man has chosen an ox as his dance ox, he will work its horns into perfect symmetry or any whimsical shape that takes his fancy. This is done (*left*) by throwing the animal to the ground, breaking its boss with a heavy stone and manipulating the horns in the desired way.

Should a man kill many enemies in his lifetime, he will cut a serration on the ears of his dance ox (*above left*)

LEFT AND ABOVE: Some men will burn stripes and circles on the flanks and shoulders of a steer with a special branding iron when it is still two or three months old. As it matures, it takes on the appearance of a strange wild animal, half bovine and half zebroid. The purpose behind all this effort is for a man to own a unique and instantly recognizable dance ox which he names after one of its quirks. His friends will call him by the same name. When charging into battle, he will gain courage by yelling its name at the top of his voice.

LEFT, RIGHT, AND FOLLOWING PAGES: At the end of a dance session, the participants enjoy the song of the bulls. The girls toss back their heads and swirl their skirts as the men jump into the air by flexing their ankles in a seemingly effortless way. Then, each man in turn takes centre stage in the circle and extols in song the wonders of his dance ox. He will explain how it came into his possession, its pedigree, where it usually grazes, its hue, its distinguishing traits and, with outstretched arms, imitate the shape of its horns. Once the other dancers are satisfied that the description fits exactly the ox owned by the soloist, they join in, first the men followed by the women who approach him one by one, tossing their plaited locks toward him with a flick of the head as if to say 'I am the one for you'. Finally, the man leaps high in the air with knees stiff, body erect and head back as if alluding to the fierceness of his beast, before returning to the circle to allow the next person to extol the virtues of another ox. Every Turkana male, from initiation to death, will have an *emong'* (dance ox) of his own.

Women and girls are responsible for watering stock which is unusual among pastoralists. Cattle are trained to go two days without water and travel great distances to and from good pasture. They are more likely to succumb through weakness from lack of grazing than from disease.

LEFT: Work at the waterholes can be arduous. In the dry season, the water table drops, and three or more pairs of hands may be needed to lift water to the stock troughs. Sometimes, a girl working a deep water-hole will kiss the water containers on every fill as a form of prayer to Akuj, who is the supreme being and creator of all things past and present, hoping the trickle will not run dry before all her family's stock is satisfied.

FAR LEFT: Tultul is a permanent rock pool in the foothills of the Uganda Escarpment. The Turkana herdsmen who use it have to be well armed to deter stock rustling. Though speaking the same language as the Turkana, the Karamajong and Dodoth who live across the border in Uganda, are age-old enemies of the Turkana and frequently clash with them for possession of livestock.

Women and children routinely milk their family's herds. They must never mix the milk from two animals in the same milking vessel although all of it can be poured into one large bowl or gourd. The art of milking the rather small, humped-back, zebu cattle the Turkana own is never to milk an animal dry.

RIGHT: Even at the best times of year, cows do not produce much more than three pints of milk a day, so the family's diet has to be supplemented with blood. Both cattle and camels are bled through the jugular vein using a bow and short, sharp arrows. Sheep and goats may also be bled by making a small incision with an arrowhead under the eye. The blood is stirred vigourously to stop it coagulating. It may be drunk on its own or mixed with milk.

Milk containers are regularly sterilized with smoke from an aromatic wood or dry herbs. The milk will have a smokey flavour, especially if left for two days in the container to curdle like yoghurt. Camels' milk takes five days longer than cows' milk to curdle. Wooden milking vessels are rinsed out with cow's urine. Pots for keeping butter, fat or honey are made from cylindrical boughs of hollowed-out wood covered at either end with tight-fitting leather caps. Camel hide is preferred for making *akitom*, the large leather containers used for storing fat.

At about the age of four, boys will begin to herd their families' kids and lambs under the watchful eye of their parents. Within two or three years, they will become responsible for the calves and young camels or the flocks of sheep and goats. Charge of the mature camels comes next at about the age of twelve followed a year or two later by cattle – their families' most valued possession.

BELOW: Girls walk to the nearest hole with wood-hewn stock watering troughs balanced on their heads. When they have finished this daily chore, they must take the troughs home. They are never left at the waterhole in case of an enemy raid.

A young boy herds his father's goats to water. While cattle are trained to go two days without water, goats must be watered every day.

BELOW: Despite their immaturity, young girls will help their mothers water their families' small stock. Boys of the same age will control the flocks at the waterhole, only allowing animals to drink in groups of ten or so at a time.

LEFT AND BELOW: The deep, rain-filled rock pools at Sirima, close to the eastern shores of the lake, are a vital dry weather watering place for the large herds of sheep and goats that graze and browse the desolate terrain. Ancient rock engravings can be seen a short distance from the pools. Some of them are now forty feet above present ground level.

ABOVE: Camels can be milked on average five times a day, and will be bled when food is scarce. They go without water for two weeks at a time and browse waterless areas where no other domestic animals can survive. In the cultural sense, however, their significance is limited. They are of a uniformly drab hue; they have no horns to manipulate; they cannot replace a wedding ox; and above all, no Turkana man in his right mind would ever dream of singing a camel's praises.

RIGHT: The Turkana are one of the few tribes in East Africa to take precautions against famine. They know from experience that they cannot afford to ignore natural disasters which loom large and occasionally overwhelm them. In a good wet season when milk is plentiful, women will boil and beat the surplus, then spread it thinly over clean cowhides to dry in the sun. The resultant dried or crusted milk, *edodo*, will be kept for their children in emergencies.

146

A young herdsboy sneaks a drink of milk straight from a camel's udder. Malnutrition is rare among stockowners.

An old woman shells the edible fruits of *Boscia coriacea*, an evergreen shrub which is widespread in Kenya'a dry bush country. Her receptacle is the shell of a small leopard tortoise which is a favoured food of the local people. Fossil remains prove that, two million years ago, giant tortoises, closely allied to the species in the Galapogos Islands and Aldabra, were common in the area but became extinct, possibly due to predation from man.

RIGHT AND BELOW: Doum palm trees are 'owned' by individual familes under a system of traditional user rights. The nuts have a 30 per cent protein content and form an important part of the Turkana diet. The outside skin is removed, pounded and boiled with water into a gruel while the nut is crushed, mixed with blood and dried for later use.

ABOVE: Nomadic communities are very clever at making the best use of nature's gifts. Trees are a vital resource to the Turkana providing fruit, pods, nuts, medicines, dry season fodder for small stock, firewood and raw material for liquid containers and utensils. A careful balance is maintained between exploitation and conservation. This young girl is shaking the branches of an acacia tree with a long stick to remove the ripe pods. These are an important feed for goats.

RIGHT: The Ng'ikebootok are a territorial section of the Turkana who are hunter-gatherers and own no stock. Living beside the Turkwell River where they supplement their food by small-scale subsistence cultivation, they otherwise live on plant food, honey, termites and wild animals. They are the only members of their tribe to keep beehives and harvest honey, and are a rare example of man exploiting but not destroying his environment. The hives are made from hollowed-out boughs which are positioned in tall trees.

ABOVE: The Uganda Escarpment is a conspicuous feature marking the international boundary between Kenya and Uganda. It is the western wall of the Central Rift Valley system, sometimes called the Gregory Rift Valley, where the land rises steeply 3000 to 5000 feet above the low-lying Turkana plains.

LEFT: Leopard in the foothills of the Uganda escarpment.

FAR LEFT: The traditional weaponry of the Turkana consists of a long shafted spear with a narrow blade, a small rectangular shield made of giraffe or buffalo hide, a wrist knife worn round the assailant's right wrist, and one or two finger knives for gouging out an enemy's eyes. The young men were an awesome sight in full battle cry.

FAR RIGHT: Musical instruments are rare in Turkana culture. The *Aburuch* is a long trumpet primarily used as a warhorn. Made from the hollowed-out bough of the *etesiro* shrub (*Gomocarpus fruticosus*) and sheathed in thick skin, it is seldom seen in today's conflicts which rely on modern firepower. Retired Chief Lobuno has owned this fine instrument for more than thirty years.

RIGHT: The British banned the making or wearing of finger knives during colonial rule because these little weapons were considered so lethal in close-combat fights.

BELOW: A bracelet made from the talons of a black kite. This bird of prey is widespread in East and Central Africa. The Turkana trap it by putting a morsel of raw meat on the tip a spear blade, and hide themselves flat on the ground. As the bird swoops to take the meat, they thrust the spear upwards. Timing needs to be perfect!

BELOW, RIGHT: A superbly crafted cartridge belt made of oryx hide. The Turkana are gifted marksmen and have wonderful eyesight.

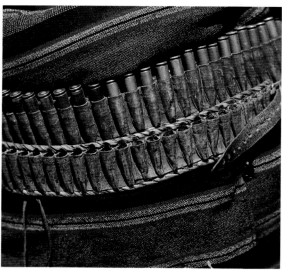

Fights using razor-sharp wrist knives and finger knives are uncommon because the injuries inflicted by them can be very severe. These young men are merely sparring.

RIGHT: Modern weapons have replaced those used in traditional warfare near the troubled regions bordering the Sudan and Uganda. Civil wars in those countries have led to a ready availability of dangerous firearms, foremost of which is the Russian Kalashnikov AK47 assault rifle such as the one this little boy is carrying to his father.

5

Ceremonies and Celebrations

THE NOMADIC LIFESTYLE of the Turkana has caused people to adopt a less rigid age-grade system than other pastoral communities in East Africa. The transition from boyhood to manhood is celebrated by one ceremony, called *asapan*. The transition from childhood to womanhood is simply by marriage. While most pastoralists in the region view circumcision as an extremely important rite of passage, the Turkana look upon the practice with disdain.

Central to every rite of passage by the Turkana is the slaughter of animals and the smearing of the participants with chyme (*Ngikujit*) – the partially digested grass from the stomach of a slaughtered animal. Stockless families cannot partake unless they borrow an animal from others, or raid their enemies' herds. The conduct of the rituals highlights the enormous significance of livestock in their society. The use of chyme can best be described as a blessing to protect the person undergoing the rite. Chyme is a substance in transition from one state to another just like the people on whose bodies it is smeared. It makes them cool, removing any anxiety they may have about their new status. Although the practice is unusual elsewhere, its application is a tradition among the Ateger-speaking peoples.

Male initiation

All Turkana youths undergo an *asapan* ceremony, which is as important to them as circumcision is to others. It confers an age-set name and full adult status on young men. Before *asapan*, boys have no standing in the tribe and are treated as juveniles. They undergo the ritual between the ages of twelve and eighteen, depending on their fathers' age grade and status. After it is over, they become protectors of the family herds, choose an ox and sing its praises at dances, join stock raids, and as soon as economic circumstances permit, marry. Customarily, a young man is not allowed to marry before completing his *asapan*. However, this rule has now been relaxed. With changing lifestyles, the ceremony is losing its importance and will most likely die out.

The ritual is organized by cattle brand divisions with the oldest living members from each setting the date. Timing depends on the phase of the moon and the propitious siting of the morning star, *Etopkile*, and the evening star, *Etopberu*. The Turkana perceive *Etopkile* as a male star and consequently the more auspicious of the two. The first to perform the ceremony are members of the Kamatak cattle brand division, the largest in the tribe.

Providing the rains are bountiful, the area is peaceful, and no prominent old men have died, *asapan* may be held annually. In practice, drought and famine can delay it for three or four years at a time with boys continually pestering their fathers to get on with the arrangements. In the months leading up to the ritual, boys go around with long rawhide whips and fight other youths, sometimes in jest, but often in earnest. In the past, stick fights were not unusual either, but they are no longer in vogue. The combatants protected themselves with wicker shields of the same shape and size as war shields which are made of thick hide.

Since the nomadic life of the Turkana precludes large gatherings, each ceremony is performed for between two and twenty boys. Families meet at the chosen site – usually a sacred tree – the day before the ceremony is due to take place. Each initiate will have a guardian who looks after him for several weeks at the conclusion of the ritual. Elders are keen to persuade respected and well-disciplined boys to stay with them because family ties remain strong. When the boy marries, his guardian gives him an ox.

LEFT: A young man with a braided hairstyle. The scarification on his right shoulder denotes that he has already killed an enemy.

Dancing may continue into the early hours of the morning while the elders feast. In the morning, they assemble in a semicircle under the sacred tree, facing east. Women and girls are not allowed to witness the ceremony. They sing and dance on their own, well out of sight. Like so many ceremonies of nomadic communities, there are local variations to the rite.

The senior elder in charge of *asapan* orders the initiates to divide between their moieties and form two lines in order of their fathers' seniority. That will be the order of their own seniority in their respective cattle brand divisions for the rest of their lives. Each boy leads his male animal for slaughter with his guardian by his side. Although oxen are preferred, not many families can afford them these days, so most make do with a camel or a goat. The boys, naked by now, kill their animals in turn by spearing them through the heart from the right side. Their guardians hold their right hands to assist them aim. Each boy has a helper from the age-set immediately senior to him to butcher his animal.

First, the belly is slit open and the intestines removed. The stomach is then cut and the contents tipped out. The senior elder walks slowly down the line of boys smearing the head, shoulders, chest, stomach and thighs of each of them with chyme. When he has finished, the elders will bless the initiates by spitting on them through pursed lips first water, then milk, and finally the masticated pulp of the young roots of the *Salvadora persica* tree. Afterwards, the boys regroup in their separate moieties and sit with outstretched legs facing east behind the old men. They must not look over their shoulders until the ceremony is over.

Meanwhile, the boys' helpers light a large communal fire and place all the animals on top of it until their skins are scorched by the flames and become taut. Next, the animals are cut up without removing the skin, and the joints roasted over the glowing embers. Every morsel has to be cooked except the right hind legs. These remain beside the open stomach sacks and will be eaten by the oldest living elders in the locality of the ceremony the following day. The rest of the meat must be divided according to tradition with the oldest men there receiving the best cuts. They eat in the semicircle they formed at the start of the ritual, still facing east.

Each guardian will put a part of the liver of his 'godson's' animal to the boy's lips. The boy will bite off a small piece and spit it out. Immediately afterwards, he takes the liver in his right hand, and eats it. Later, he is given the backbone of his animal with practically no meat on the bone. Then, he will be handed the femur from its front left leg, and jointly with his guardian breaks it with one blow from a heavy stone.

The boys must not bend their knees when their guardians pull them upright towards the end of the feasting. They lead them to where their wives and daughters have waited patiently to shave hair from the front and sides of the boys' heads. (Until *asapan*, boys plait their hair in a range of styles.) After being anointed with a mixture of animal fat and charcoal, the boys return to their original places where their guardians, or guardians' sons if they have completed their *asapan*, fashion their hair with clay. The shape of the clay bun is peculiar to this ceremony and resembles a close fitting skullcap. Moreover, the clay is not coloured with the customary blue pigment so typical of the tribe. A small tassel made from the tendons of the animal each boy killed is tied to the hair at the back of the crown. After the important ritual is over, the initiates will celebrate their adulthood by singing and dancing with men of the age-set immediately senior to them.

On the third and last day of the ceremony, every article of dress, weaponry, or ornamentation an initiate ever possessed will be taken by his guardian and replaced with new ones. Afterwards, they leave together for his homestead where the boy will be led round by the hand like a child, all the while being asked to name common objects, such as livestock, household utensils, weapons and so on, which are pointed out to him by his guardian. The boy looks after the livestock for the duration of his stay and in return for this help, his guardian will give him a cow, a camel, or up to four goats depending on his guardian's wealth. When the boy goes home, his gift must be handed to his father who may pass it on to the boy's mother.

Once the proud young man has bought himself a brace of new spears, he will be anxious to prove himself in the excitement of a stock raid. If he kills an enemy, he will be undergo special scarification to manifest his bravery.

Marriage

Marriage marks an important milestone in Turkana life. Every man will marry first when he is between twenty and thirty years old, and depending on his wealth, again after middle age. Turkana wealth is related solely to livestock, and, as polygamists, men build up their herds in order to marry as many wives as possible.

Young men can tell their fathers if they have a preference for a girl, though arranged marriages are more typical. The boy's mother will always be consulted as she has a better understanding of a girl's character and capacity for work. Girls marry at fifteen to eighteen and are rarely allowed a choice of spouses. Although a father may ask his daughter's opinion, he could overrule her, especially if the man is rich. The girl's only ways of objecting would be to run away, or threaten to commit suicide. Younger men do not necessarily make ideal husbands as older men are generally wealthier. Also, a man's other wives mean companionship and shared work for the girl.

Marriage is unlikely between families whose economic circumstances are very different, where there are already close marital ties, or where livestock has identical brand markings to those of the other family's herds. As brand markings are regulated by divisions within the tribe, this restriction prevents distant relatives unknowingly marrying each other.

Fifty years ago, the average number of animals a man had to amass for the bride wealth was thirty plus one head of cattle, fifteen camels, and eighty-five to three hundred sheep and goats. A donkey was the equivalent of fifteen goats. Today, a very wealthy stockowner may pay a similar bride wealth, but the majority of families will settle for far less because their economic circumstances are so different from those of past generations. Nevertheless, the essence of a marriage is the transfer of stock (except among the hunter gatherer's) and nothing else will do. A long time ago payment by instalments was not permitted, but this is now commonplace.

The complex marriage ritual consists of a marriage agreement and the ceremony itself. The first stage of the agreement is accomplished when the young man's father goes alone to the girl's father to ask for his daughter. Although the girl's name is not mentioned, the intended bride is obvious. The conversation can often be very obscure. The visitor may say that he has come to beg a fine ox. The girl's father will retort that his ox is young and small. After talking in riddles for a while, the visitor will be dismissed with the words: 'I have heard you speak. Now you may go.' Being abrupt and non-committal, the girl's father leaves all his options open. However, there is also comfort for the young man. If the bride's father disapproved of the match, he would have made it abundantly clear and nothing more could be done.

It may take several weeks for the girl's family to make up their minds. Intermediaries keep the young man and his father informed of the discussions, but in the end, unnerving silence signifies their agreement. Once the suitor is sure, he will gather friends and relatives of his own age to escort him to the girl's homestead. At least two-thirds of his party will be girls, and all will dress in their finery. The purpose of this visit is to present chewing tobacco and a fat ram or billy goat to the girl's father. These gifts are received in a perfunctory manner and pushed to one side. He has little idea of his future father-in-law's true feelings because the party must leave quickly. Nor will he speak to the girl; though he will know all about her, he may not have ever seen her.

After three or four days, the girl's father calls his age-mates to discuss the merits of the young man. If they oppose the match, the gifts are returned. If they accept, one of the old men whose eldest daughter is already properly married, will open the tobacco. First he throws a pinch into the fire burning in the hearth of the girl's mother's hut; both her parents are then given a little, then some is given to the rest of the elders present.

Word is sent to the young man who will rejoice: his gift has been opened, a sign for him to gather boys of his own age. They decorate their clay hairdos with their best ostrich feathers to accompany him and his male relatives to the girl's homestead to negotiate the bride wealth. By tradition, they stop short of the main entrance where each wife of the bride's father will be promised a cow or a camel with calf at heel. This pledge can never be forgotten, waived, or varied.

Negotiations take hours. Each side haggles skilfully, attempting to force the other to yield. The more a family can afford, the more is demanded of them and the more they must give way. The young man usually promises the girl's paternal uncles two to five cows, her father's eldest sister one cow, one camel, ten goats, and a fat sheep, and gifts for the girl's namesake and other relatives away from the home. The girl's father will receive two bulls and one calf, and much else later.

Once the two families agree, the young man and his entourage escort the girl's parents and relatives back to his father's homestead where the bride wealth will be given out to seal the marriage. The young man and girl are now bride and groom even though the bride has remained at her parents' home in case a last minute objection arose over the composition of the stock. The bride's parents and relatives must hurry home with the animals so that the elders may bless them before the new owners take their share.

The groom's party, including his mother and sisters, follow closely to collect the costly bride. The groom carries the tanned hide of a white bull and a small wooden container of powdered limestone. The hide is laid out on the floor of the bride's mother's house and white powder is sprinkled on it. Then the bride and groom stand on it in the centre of the homestead, facing east. They leave after the bride's parents bless the couple by smearing their faces and chests with the remains of the powder mixed with a little water. The bride must not set foot there again until the groom slaughters the wedding ox which he must provide.

Many years may elapse between a marriage agreement and the wedding ceremony, while the couple live as man and wife. The ceremonies may also be combined. The decision rests with the groom and his ability to pay off the bride wealth. It is a golden rule that there can be no wedding ceremony unless all the livestock promises have been fully discharged. Nor may a man marry another wife until he has completed the ritual slaughter of the wedding ox for his first wife. The wedding ox may be an animal of any reasonable size as long as it has horns.

Weddings are great festive occasions, and usually take place in the wet season when there is enough food for a large gathering of guests. The date is set by the groom and his best friends. Though fully aware of the preparations, the bride's family are given very little warning of the actual day. I attended a wedding when the suitor turned up three days later than expected, but nobody cared. Guests talked endlessly and slept without much thought of food.

Early on the wedding morning, the groom leaves his homestead with his close friends and relatives to drive the wedding ox, and at least five sheep and three goats, to his father-in-law's home. A donkey or two laden with water will follow as they must pause a short distance east of their destination to water the ox.

Soon, the bride's friends and relatives bar the groom's way to allow any relative who has yet to receive a share of the bride wealth one final opportunity to press claims. There is nothing polite about this as I discovered at Nachola. The groom was taunted as he sat patiently on his stool surrounded by relatives and friends. I heard a man shout, 'Do not waste our time. Stand up and tell us if we are to be given what we have asked for or go home!' The tone was belligerent, but it was more in jest than in anger, for the groom knew exactly what was expected of him, and the bride's relatives are bound by recognized custom.

Once women from the bride's homestead have been paid for building a rough hut where meat from the wedding ox is kept, the ceremony can begin. The ox is driven into a special enclosure close to the hut. The groom then gives the oldest man present of his own age-set some chewing tobacco to be put into a cow-horn container, and divided among the assembled elders. Next, a man is chosen to kill the ox by spearing it through the heart from its right side. Others position themselves with spears at the ready in case the elder misses, and the animal bolts. As the ox sags to its knees, the old men intone a blessing so it will collapse on its left side, otherwise it must be quickly rolled over. If blood oozes from its nostrils, the bride has to undergo a cleansing ritual the next day to ward off evil spirits, and the possibility of her becoming barren.

The elders butcher the ox with their spears, first cutting out the fat round its testicles and rear underbelly. This must be made into necklaces for the bride's father, and three or four respected old men that afternoon. The man who removes this fat will mutter a threat: if the bride sleeps with any man other than her husband, she, her children, or her animals will die.

The ox blood is collected in a wooden vessel and put to one side. Should the bridegroom already be married, his eldest wife must come forward and tie the windpipe and main artery leading to the stomach four times each. Otherwise it is believed the new bride will not bear children. If he has more than one wife, the others will wash the ox's stomach with water.

As the animal is carved up, each portion is carried to the wedding hut surrounded by singers. The horns of the ox, attached together by a small strip of head skin, are placed on top of the hut and must remain there until the hut collapses, and they drop to the ground. The homestead may not move until this happens. Five ribs from the right and six ribs from the left side of the animal, and the shin from its right front leg will be put to one side. These will be roasted and eaten later in the day by elders of the bride's family, east of the homestead. The rest of the meat will be boiled and served that evening or the following day.

Once the butchering is complete, the elders of the bride's family are called in order of seniority to drink the blood of the wedding ox mixed with sugar and milk. The bride's family also take in their right hands a little chyme from the ox's stomach and smear it over themselves to bless the bride. The groom and his party are not involved in this ritual and do not partake of the blood.

The elders leave the stock pen singing, preceded by the bride's male relatives and friends. The groom will present them with two sheep and a goat, and join them a short distance from the homestead as they slaughter the animals, and roast them whole in their skin. The men eat sitting in a semicircle according to their moieties, the leopards, *ng'irisae*, on the right and the mountains, *ng'imor*, on the left. Their spears are kept by their right sides with the blades pointing inwards towards the fire.

Female friends and relatives of the bride are not ignored. Outside the wedding hut they will cook two sheep given to them by the groom. Those who built the hut will collect the head, stomach, and the offal of the wedding ox, including the heart, lungs, kidneys and liver. These will be boiled with a morsel from every other part of the animal except the shin bone from its front right leg. Later, they will supplement this food with one of their sheep. The bride's mother and stepmothers wear around their necks a strip of fat from the ox's stomach to signify their status. They throw meat to the other women who are expressly forbidden to handle it until it is safely caught in their leather aprons. The woman whose husband speared the wedding ox is the only one spared this custom.

Singing and dancing continues the whole afternoon, the male dancers rewarded by the groom with a fat sheep or goat. Towards sunset, the bride and groom move near the wedding hut for the final blessing, the only occasion that day when the bride participates in the ceremony. The groom is joined by his brothers, any of his other wives, and his closest friends. The blessing will be conducted by a close male relative of the bride. The couple stand on a cow or oxhide from an animal killed for eating, not one that died from disease or old age. As they face east, the old man smears them, and the others present, with a paste of powdered limestone, then intones a blessing. They are now officially husband and wife.

Next day, the bride's father will give the groom's family more food — yet another sheep or goat to mark the pegging out of the oxhide inside the wedding hut by the bride's mother and friends. In four or five days time, when the hide is completely dry, they will scrape all the little scraps of dried flesh from it. These will be boiled and eaten with the ox's hooves and dried stomach which they had put previously to one side. Later, the leather from the lower front legs of the hide will be cut off, and the rest prepared as a sleeping mat for the bride's parents. The two leg pieces will be sewn either side of the bride's rear skirt if it is customary for women of her husband's cattle brand division to do so.

As the new bride nears her husband's home the day after the wedding, his relatives and close friends come to greet her, offering gifts of livestock. When the marriage agreement and the wedding ceremony take place years apart, this stock is given to her at the conclusion of the marriage agreement. Likewise, she may already be wearing the attire of a married woman. If she is not, her mother-in-law and co-wives or husband's sisters will give it to her. In turn, she will share the beads and decorations of her unmarried status with the young girls of her husband's family.

She and her husband spend their first night in the house of his senior wife should he be married already, or in his mother's house if he is not. A small child will be loaned to her to nurse as a symbol of her future fertility.

When a man marries another wife, the views of the first wife are paramount. If she disapproves of the choice, her husband can do nothing. It is not unusual for a man who already has three or four wives, to marry a girl who is forty years his junior. Should he die when she is still young, arrangements will be made for her, with her consent, to become the wife of another member of the family. This person is likely to be one of her late husband's younger brothers or the son of a senior wife.

If a young wife is unfaithful, it is firmly believed that her children or livestock will die. In order to cleanse herself from evil, the unfaithful wife has to beg a bull from her father for slaughter at her husband's homestead. As she and her lover walk naked round the perimeter of the homestead slowly scattering its chyme behind them, her husband and his friends give them a resounding beating with thin, whip-like sticks. The *elomit* is a humiliating and painful experience which men and women rarely want to repeat.

Divorce is extremely rare among the Turkana. Even barrenness is not an acceptable grounds for separation. In such cases, the unfortunate woman will bring up children given to her by her co-wives as her own.

The strict rules regarding the slaughter of the wedding ox have been relaxed these days, though a man still has to give at least three-quarters of the bride wealth he had promised the girls' parents before the ceremony can take place. A prolonged delay can be to his disadvantage. If one of his daughters attains marriageable age before he has slaughtered his wife's wedding ox, the girl's bride wealth will be taken by his in-laws. There is nothing he can do about this unless he finalizes the arrangements of his own wedding first.

Although he cannot marry again until the wedding ox of his first wife has been slaughtered, he may take a concubine. Since the woman is not married to him, he has no legal right to their children or redress if she chooses to be unfaithful. In customary law, the children belong to the girl's parents who demand a fine for each child she bears. This makes it increasingly difficult for him ever to marry her. The status of concubines can never be kept secret because they do not wear the attire of married women. Although their back skirts are identical, their front aprons resemble those of young girls.

Childbirth

Childbirth takes place outside a woman's home assisted by two traditional midwives, surrounded by other women. One midwife holds her shoulders while the other massages her stomach. If the baby is a boy, a pinch of tobacco is put into the mother's fire before the umbilical cord is tied with fibre from the *edome* tree (*Cordia sinensis*), and cut with the blade of a spear. The placenta is wrapped in leaves from the same tree and buried in the family's goatpen. If it is a baby girl, the umbilical cord is cut with a knife. The placenta, wrapped in the leaves of *eerut* (*Maaerua decumbens*), is buried behind her mother's home. The woman is confined for four days if she gives birth to a boy and three days for a girl during which time she must avoid all contact with the family's livestock.

Four goats are slaughtered over a twenty-four-hour period to celebrate the birth although the roasted meat and soup made from the carcass may only be eaten cold. The Turkana believe the unpalatable food prevents the child becoming a glutton in later life. The skin from the first animal, *anapet*, will be tanned and sewn into a pouch for carrying the child on its mother's back. If childbirth is difficult, and the woman is in labour for long, her husband will slit a goat's throat while two men hold it high in the air. The labouring woman must crawl under it four times, allowing blood to drip on her as she does so. Chyme is then smeared on her forehead and stomach. This is believed to ease the birth without further complication.

A child is given a name at birth associated with an event taking place at the time: for example, rain, famine or a raid. The real name is given at sunrise the next morning when the last of the four goats is killed. The child is named after a living person who solicits the mother to use his name. If she agrees, and the child suckles when the name is called, he will be entitled to an ox.

Death

Death is an important rite of passage for elderly, respected members of the community and the ceremonies surrounding the demise of the head of a family are arguably the most complex of all in Turkana culture. They last seven days. This is an indication of the esteem in which a man is held by his family and friends. In contrast, the death of an unmarried man or woman, or a child, is taken lightly, and the bodies are left in the bush for hyenas to devour.

If the family head is seriously ill, he must refrain from discussing topics related to his animals, food, grazing, water or raids. When he feels his end is drawing near, he must summon his eldest brother or his eldest son. He tells the man to look after his household and his wives after his death. He also reminds his senior wife of her responsibilities towards his children. Moments before he dies, the wife begins to wail. She leaves the hut as soon as he is dead to gather grass. She stuffs the grass into a large wooden milk container with embers from her own fire. After shaking it vigorously, she pushes her late husband's head briefly into the smoke.

Relatives and members of his extended family gather round to console the bereaved while the dead man's brothers and grown-up sons dig a grave in the family's goatpen. The intense heat necessitates a quick burial. The widows strip the body of all its ornaments and clothing. They then wrap it in a white oxhide, and holding the lower part of the body, help his sons carry it to the grave where it is gently lowered, facing east. Branches from the *esekon* tree (*Salvadora persica*) are laid over the body whereupon the widows turn their backs on the grave, and scoop the soil backwards between their legs with bare hands. The family's goats are then let into the pen to trample the soil into the ground. Next, stones are placed on the grave, and thorn scrub from the man's open sleeping enclosure is collapsed on top. This scrub is draped with his favourite personal belongings: his stool, tobacco pouch, walking stick and ostrich feather container. Food, milk, water and oil are put nearby.

All the married men living at the deceased's homestead leave home for four days while the widows of the deceased participate in a series of intricate rituals assisted by an old woman beyond child-bearing age, known as *aketuluron* (the head shaver). On the fifth day, the deceased's eldest brother, failing which his eldest son, takes over as head of the family. He will use a spear to kill the old man's favourite 'dance ox' to the west of the animal enclosures. On the seventh day the family moves home. One more goat is slaughtered, and an offering is left on top of the grave to appease the spirits of the deceased.

Eleven moons later – roughly a year – a final ceremony is held in memory of the deceased. It is a joyous occasion with several animals being slaughtered by the senior widow's eldest son. At the end of the ceremony, this man assumes full responsibility for the homestead. The numerous restrictions associated with death are now lifted to enable the family to resume a normal life: the prohibition on the widows braiding their hair is removed; their daughters can be married; *asapan* ceremonies can be held; and cattle can be branded or exchanged once more.

Families must maintain good relations with their ancestors for their wellbeing. Illness is thought to be caused by a dead relative who has not been appeased. There are many reasons why the dead can return to haunt the living. Evil spirits might manifest themselves as snakes, frogs, lions and hyenas, or ghosts who light fires on hilltops, and sing at night. They have to be appeased regularly with offerings and prayers, and by a stranger placing green foliage or a pinch of tobacco on top of a grave when he passes it. As the man does so, he will mutter the words: 'Rest in peace. Do not haunt me'.

ABOVE AND LEFT: Before youths are initiated, they are not allowed to style their hair in the distinctive clay bun of mature Turkana men. Instead, they braid their hair in several different ways, sometimes coating it with animal fat and adding red ochre to colour the braids.

BELOW: The Turkana stool prevents damage to the clay hairdo during rest.

ABOVE AND PREVIOUS PAGES: In the months leading up to their intiation ceremonies, youths engage each other in rawhide whip fights to test their courage and ability to withstand pain. The whips can inflict terrible weals on their backs and shoulders.

RIGHT: This fierce looking young man is wearing wooden charms on one of his necklaces to protect himself from injury.

LEFT: Each initiate will have a helper to roast the male animal he slaughters with his spear at the start of the *asapan* ceremony. These animals are roasted on a communal fire without removing the skin.

ABOVE: Initiates also have guardians with whom they stay after the ritual is over. The guardian puts a part of the liver of his 'godson's' animal to the boy's lips. The boy bites off a small piece and spits it out. He will then take hold of the remains and eat it, while sitting with outstretched legs facing east.

BELOW: Animal blood is collected in a wooden bowl and drunk by the assembled elders. They sit in a semicircle facing east under a sacred tree.

The senior elder in charge of *asapan* blesses the intiates by smearing each one of them on the forehead, chest and stomach with chyme.

RIGHT: As the *asapan* ceremony draws to a close, the guardians fashion their 'godson's' hair into a clay bun which resembles a close fitting skullcap. It is not coloured with the customary blue pigment. A small tassel made from the tendons of the boy's animal is tied to the hair at the back of the crown.

BELOW AND RIGHT: The most significant scarification a man will undergo is called *akiger*. It is applied by an elder to someone who has killed an enemy in battle, and has a witness to the feat. The entire right side of his chest, back and shoulder will be scarred in neat rows. Should the man kill a woman in a raid, the scarification will be done to the left side of his body only. If he kills many enemies in his lifetime, the left side of his body will be scarred after his right side; this will be followed by his right biceps, and lastly his left. When there is no room for any more scarring, his attention turns to his eldest sister who will have her right shoulder, then her left shoulder, and lastly her abdomen below the rib cage scarred. If he kills more enemies in his lifetime, he will cut the ears of his dance ox in a serrate pattern.

Scarification is a painful experience. A girl will sit in front of the man to make sure he does not cringe or show any outward signs of pain. It is customary for the singed and blackened hairs scraped from the tail of a roasted sheep to be rubbed into the open wounds. Later, cow fat is applied to help the healing process.

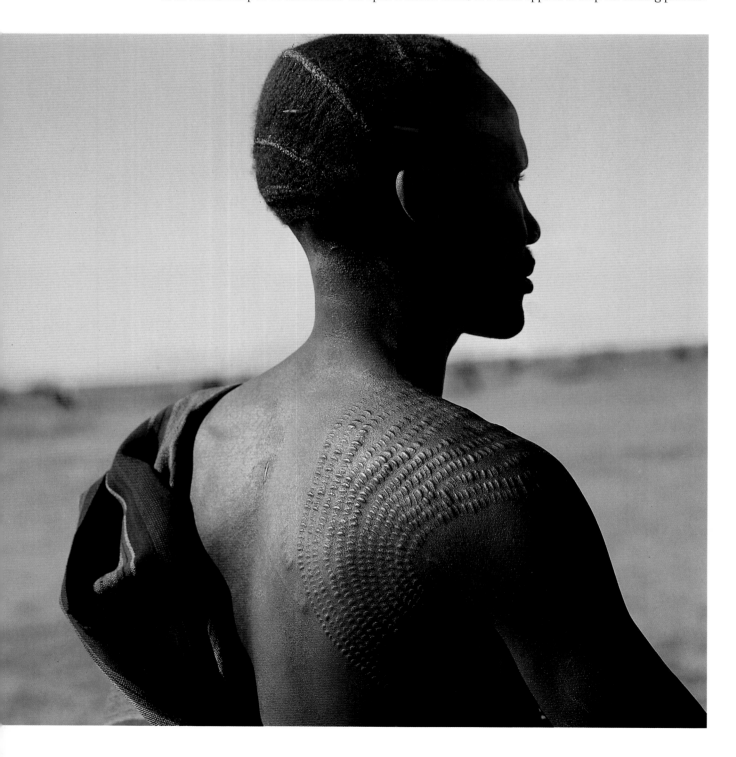

While a woman of the bride's family (*left*) watches over the wedding preparations, the groom (*above*) drives a part of the agreed bride wealth toward the home of his future parents-in-law. He must bring with him the wedding ox, *ekumae*, which will be slaughtered and eaten that day. The composition of the bride wealth is related directly to the wealth of the groom and his immediate family, especially the size of their herds.

179

ABOVE AND RIGHT: As the groom approaches, driving a part of the agreed bride wealth before him, women from the bride's homestead sing and dance, menacing his party while his female supporters raise their sticks, and push them away. The confrontation looks ugly, but it is all good fun. The purpose of it is to extract as many promises of stock from the groom as possible before the wedding begins. He will customarily give them the only nanny goat he has brought with him, which must not have given birth.

Weddings are great festive occasions and anyone may attend. They generally take place toward the end of a wet season when food is plentiful for the large gathering of guests. July – *Losuban* (the month of plenty) in the Turkana calendar – is the preferred month.

BELOW: The wedding ox is speared by a chosen elder through the heart from its right side. As it sags to its knees, the old men bless it to collapse on its left side; otherwise it must be rolled over quickly.

RIGHT: The elders butcher the ox with their spears, first cutting out the fat around its testicles and rear underbelly, which will be made into necklaces for the bride's father and other respected old men.

Marriage is a cause for celebration. Singing and dancing will continue well into the night.

At the end of the day, the groom confers with his friends (*above*) before he and his bride are blessed (*right*) by an elder, who smears them with a paste of powdered limestone.

ABOVE: Twins are a blessing. However, one child will always be cared for by a foster mother, possibly a co-wife beyond child-bearing age. Until they can walk, a proud mother wears a plain, wide leather neckband, and numerous bangles round her wrists and forearms to signify her status. Mothers among some cattle brand divisions of the tribe refuse to speak to strangers unless they first receive a gift.

LEFT: When a woman gives birth, four goats will be slaughtered in a twenty-four-hour period to celebrate the occasion. The skin of the first goat is made into a pouch for carrying the baby on its mother's back. Note the small wooden balls on a string, attached to the pouch. They are charms to ward off evil spirits.

Song is an art form ingrained in Turkana culture. Songs in praise of cattle or brave warriors who defend their herds and raid are just one aspect of it, albeit an important one. People sing about love, hate, good fortune and misery. They sing to entertain and take inspiration from folklore. Melodious songs praise the huge stature of the elephant, the ferocity of the lion and leopard, and the speed, grace and beauty of the ostrich. Other songs praise the countryside, the mountains, the trees and the birds. Birds are not just objects to be eaten or providers of feathers for festive occasions. They are prophets of rain, forewarners of trouble, guides for wild honey, and harbingers of good and bad. There is a song for every species of bird in Turkanaland. Contrary to those who suggest that pastoralists have a narrow, bovine-orientated mentality, the Turkana have created a much wider world of their own.

RIGHT AND FOLLOWING PAGES: Young men and girls are performing the *naleyo*, the only dance among a repertoire of more than twenty where couples dance together. The songs narrate love stories about small animals such as tortoises, hares, squirrels and dikdiks.

6
Prehistory and the Lake

TURKANALAND HAS A long record of human occupation. Four million years ago, the Lake Turkana basin may have been the cradle of mankind. Human and animal remains were trapped and fossilized in the unique stratified sediments revealed by the fault lines of the Great Rift Valley. These are an incomparable record spanning more than twenty-seven million years. Since tectonic activity over the aeons has uplifted many of these ancient sediments, the constant erosion of them by wind and water exposes new finds every year to the infinite curiosity of modern man.

Dr Richard Leakey, the renowned palaeoanthropolgist, intuitively judged the hidden riches of Koobi Fora as he flew his light aircraft over the tortured terrain along the east side of Lake Turkana in 1968. Since then, teams of international scientists have combed the desiccated fossil-beds and pronounced them the richest in the world. Many thousands of fragmentary remains are perfectly preserved within sediments sandwiched between layers of volcanic ash which was ejected over a long period of intense activity. Radioactive materials in the ash or tuff decay at known rates. This makes possible the accurate dating of the layers on either side of the trapped fossils.

The startling revelations in Turkana have caused experts to revise radically their long-held views on evolution. The most significant find to date has been the 1.6 million-year-old remains of 'Turkana Boy' which were discovered east of the lake in 1984. It is the oldest and most complete skeleton of *Homo erectus* ever found and tells us more about early man than was previously known. 'Turkana Boy' has been identified as a twelve-year-old of athletic build, over six feet tall with a brain two-thirds the size of *Homo sapiens*.

Lake Turkana has been unstable throughout its known history. Periodic expansion and contraction has resulted in a complex jumble of lake, river, and delta sediments. Geologists have determined that, four million years ago, the lake was a vast expanse of freshwater, three times its present size. Little by little, drier conditions led to the closed forest of the region giving way to more open, savannah-type country teeming with game. Changes in the lake's environment are thought to have encouraged apes to adapt to a new habitat and adopt an upright posture, freeing their hands from providing the basic function of support. The lake basin is rich in specimens of *Australopithecus*, the primitive 'transitional' hominid with many ape-like features. *Australopithecus* was small-brained, bipedal, and still probably tree-climbing. However, its upright posture distinguished it from apes and put it on the first rungs of the ladder up the human family tree.

In 1995, Dr Meave Leakey, Richard's wife and herself a respected palaeoanthropologist in charge of the National Museum of Kenya research team, identified a new species of *Australopithecus* at Kanapoi, a site thirty miles from the lakeshore. This discovery, which has been given the name *anamensis*, establishes that upright posture and bipedalism go back in time beyond four million years, the earliest known stages of human evolution. Not all species of hominids are direct ancestors of modern man, for the differences between them are so great that there must have been separate lineages, only one of which could have given rise to the human race.

Koobi Fora has yielded fascinating fossils of many animals. The biodiversity in ancient times was much greater than it is today. Primitive elephants ancestral to both contemporary African and Indian elephants lived at the same time as the extinct elephant-like *Deinotherium bozasi* which had tusks only in the lower jaw. Though not living simultaneously, four distinct species of hippo were present, including a pygmy form

LEFT: Though it looks beautiful, Lake Turkana is as forbidding as its surroundings. No shoreline is barer, windier or hotter; the waters are alkaline and nauseating to drink; crocodiles lurk near its shores and huge waves can swamp a small boat.

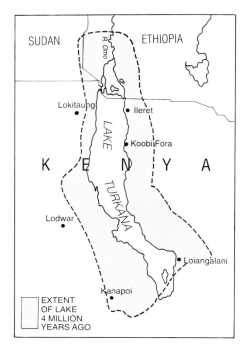

and one unknown elsewhere. Three types of giraffe roamed the wooded grasslands; two were large, one was a pygmy, and they all lived alongside the allied short-necked, long-horned, *Sivatherium maurusium*.

Crocodiles are ancient reptiles existing without much change for the last two million years. The fossils at Koobi Fora come from at least four species, including *Crocodylus niloticus*, which inhabits Lake Turkana to this day. Despite their numbers decreasing in recent years to under seven thousand, the lake is still host to one of the last great crocodile populations in the world.

Ten thousand years ago, Lake Turkana was again a large lake, stretching approximately two hundred and eighty miles from north to south and possibly covering an area of fourteen thousand square miles. There is overwhelming evidence to support a theory that this megalake was linked to the Nile basin by way of a low-level divide between the Omo plains and the Lotikipi Swamp. For this to have happened, its level would have been about 240 feet higher than it is today. Fossilized oyster shell beds embedded in sediment known as *Galana boi* and ancient rocks containing the remains of at least seven species of molluscs and eight species of fish common to the Nile system indicate that this is so. Moreover, thirty of the forty-eight species of fish found in the lake today are characteristic of species which range across the continent to West Africa. Only ten are endemic to Turkana.

Man, the predator, was drawn to the lake to hunt and fish. The earliest known pottery sites were left by communities living along the shores of the megalake about 6000 BC. Cemeteries and burial mounds of more recent inhabitants are said to date back to between 355 and 165 BC. There are two distinct cemeteries in the district; the largest is near Lokori and the other close to the Lodwar-Kalokol road, some nine miles out of Kalokol. The Turkana call both of them *Ng'amoratung'a* (the people of stone).

I know of two legends about these obscure people whose origins remain a mystery. One concerns a soothsayer whose daughters were mistreated. He punished those responsible by turning them to stone. The other relates how a grotesque wizard turned a group of dancers into stone because they laughed at his strange appearance. They are the Turkana's explanation for the rock pillars which were *in situ* long before their ancestors arrived in these arid lands. The rock is basalt which tends to weather smooth over hundreds of years. However, the nineteen pillars at the Kalokol site measuring up to three and a half feet tall are extremely smooth and well rounded at the edges. It would be surprising if they had not been worked by the hand of man. The considerable skill and effort required to put them in place is also intriguing, especially when nothing much else from the period remains except rock engravings. There are several important sites found in close proximity to an old water line when the level of the lake was much higher about 5000 to 6000 years ago. There is no way of telling if the etchings are that old. Some of the art is now forty feet above present ground level.

For more than two thousand years, the country south of the Nile Valley was the subject of great interest and speculation but the region seemed impenetrable. There were no navigable rivers, people were warlike, disease was rife, and inestimable tracts of waterless country prevented travellers journeying from most directions.

Lake Turkana — remote, mysterious and hidden in the scorching desert — was one of the last great lakes to reveal its secrets to the outside world. First mention of an unknown expanse of water lying somewhere north of Lake Baringo was made by Joseph Thomson, the Scottish explorer, who pioneered a way through Maasailand to the shores of Lake Victoria in 1884. He learnt from Jumbe Kimameta, the ivory trader who gave him a helping hand through Maasai country, of 'a great salt lake' some twenty to thirty miles wide and of unknown length. It was said to have 'surprising numbers of enormous white fish, with crocodiles and hippopotami' in its waters.

This exciting and uncommonly accurate report encouraged Count Teleki to broaden the scope of his planned hunting trip to East Africa in an attempt to find out the truth of Thomson's account. It was, after all, a time when most of Africa's treasures had been unveiled and Lake Victoria identified as the source of the Nile. The remote and mysterious lake region was one of the last remaining corners of the continent to be explored and presented Teleki with a unique challenge. He and his travelling companion, Lieutenant von Höhnel, set out from Zanzibar in January 1887 and, after fourteen months of trial and tribulation with many of their porters dying *en route*, reached the top of a volcanic ridge to describe the scene laid out before them. The date was 5 March 1888.

Von Höhnel wrote:

> For a long time we gazed in speechless delight, spell-bound by the beauty of the scene before us, whilst our men, equally silent, stared into the distance for a few minutes, to break presently into shouts of astonishment at the sight of the glittering expanse of the great lake which melted on the horizon into the blue of the sky. At that moment all our dangers, all our fatigues were forgotten in the joy of finding our exploring expedition crowned with success at last. Full of enthusiasm and gratefully remembering the gracious interest taken in our plans from the first by his Royal and Imperial Highness, Prince Rudolf of Austria, Count Teleki named the sheet of water, set like a pearl of great price in the wonderful landscape beneath us, Lake Rudolf.

In a move to rid Kenya of the last vestiges of imperialism, the Government of Kenya decreed in 1975 that the name of the lake should change to 'Turkana' though it is often referred to as the Jade Sea.

Like so many visitors who have followed in the explorers' footsteps, Teleki found his first impressions of the lake to be false. After a seven hour march over jagged lava in the intense and parching heat, they reached the lakeshore only to find the water brackish.

> This fresh defeat of all our expectations was like a revelation to us; and like some threatening spectre rose up before our minds the full significance of the utterly barren, dreary nature of the lake district. Into what a desert had we been betrayed! A few scattered tufts of fine stiff grass rising up in melancholy fashion near the shore, from the wide stretches of sand, were the only bits of green, the only signs of life of any kind. Here and there, some partly in the water, some on the beach, rose up isolated skeleton trees, stretching up in the bare, sun-bleached branches to the pitiless sky. No living creature shared the gloomy solitude with us; and far as our glass could reach there was nothing to be seen but desert – desert everywhere. To all this was added the scorching heat, and the ceaseless buffeting of the sand-laden wind, against which we were powerless to protect ourselves upon the beach, which offered not a scrap of shelter, whilst the pitching of the tents in the loose sand was quite impossible.

This description is as accurate today as it was a hundred years ago. So what attracts visitors to the lake? They are fascinated by the timeless and irresistible allure of unspoilt wilderness. The Jade Sea is a true desert lake surrounded by barren, inhospitable terrain which conjures in the mind a desolate lunar landscape. Large lava flows make walking a misery in the lake's southern hinterland where the prevailing easterly or southeasterly winds blow with greatest fury. The tendency is for strong morning winds followed by relative calm in the afternoons when the burning heat leaves you weak and panting. The sun sets in brilliant hues, and the discomfort of the day dissolves into a short period of perfect bliss. Then, the wind steadily increases again until it reaches a howling gale, gusting 50 m.p.h., by about 10 a.m. the next morning. This is caused by a system of cold air currents being drawn down from the nearby mountain tops to replace hot air which rises rapidly from the low-lying lake basin: this process is known as convection. Sometimes it is difficult to stand upright on the exposed lakeshore and the unremitting noise of rushing wind is relentless.

The abiding memory of those who know the lake well is the suddenness of the violent storms. No sane person ventures out in a small boat when the wind is blowing strongly. Heavy swells and pounding, white-plumed waves make it far too dangerous. Even if the water is seductively calm, the breeze can freshen without warning, bringing with it choppy seas that force a boat to reduce speed rapidly. Two travellers to experience the dangers of an unstable boat were John Millard and Bill Dyson, members of a 1934 expedition led by Dr Vivian Fuchs which made the first geological survey of Lake Turkana. Fuchs was later knighted for his exploration of the Antarctic.

Soon after setting off in their tiny wood and canvas boat to survey Central Island, they ran into a stiff breeze and high seas which began to drive them off course. Bailing furiously to keep the little craft afloat, they reached the island wet and exhausted late at night. The wind did not abate for five days by which time their meagre rations were almost finished. To stay alive, they fished for tilapia and stole eggs from a large colony of spoonbills nesting in one of the island's craters.

One of the highlights of the survey was the first exploration of South Island, which in the past had been known as Von Höhnel Island or Great South Island. Situated twelve miles off the southern end of the lake, the island is long and narrow, covering fifteen square miles. It is the largest of three islands which are volcanic in origin. Von Höhnel was still alive and living in Vienna as a retired admiral at the time of the expedition. He wrote to Fuchs warning him of the dangers.

> . . . It is a disquieting feeling that induces me to write to you today caused by your remark that you will endeavour to visit the Great South Island at all cost.
> I fear that I have not warned you seriously enough that you must be very careful and not underrate the risk of the enterprise. If the weather conditions are anything like they were at our time then you would be senseless to try the venture.
> I do not think that the lake at any time of the year is so calm as to be navigated with a small collapsible boat to justify any attempt to reach the island. I am therefore anxiously awaiting your news.

On 25 July, Fuchs and 'Snaffles' Martin, an expedition surveyor, made a successful crossing only to find they were not the first people to set foot on the island. Human remains, the bleached skeletons of sheep and goats, and various shards were stark evidence of the fate that had befallen a party of shipwrecked fishermen some years earlier. Even more surprising to the explorers was the sight of thirteen domestic goats in fine condition but as wild as any antelope.

Fuchs returned to the mainland three days later, leaving Martin to set about his survey. The following day Dyson, a distinguished mountaineer and the expedition doctor, left to join him with rations to last them at least ten days. Neither man was ever seen again. After an intensive search, the only small clue to their whereabouts was the discovery of the doctor's tope near the mouth of the Turkwell delta but it may have been blown there in the prevailing wind. The circumstances surrounding their death remain a mystery, but there is no doubt the flimsy boat sank without trace.

The tragedy left the island unsurveyed and added to the region's mystique. Twenty-one years elapsed before anyone set foot on the island again. George and Joy Adamson were the intrepid adventurers who found that the flocks of feral goats had multiplied to some two hundred. They came across the remains of Martin's and Dyson's camp but were unable to throw fresh light on the manner of their disappearance or death. Being seasoned safari hands, the Adamsons were prepared for any eventuality which was just as well because they were stuck on the island for eight days while the raging wind blew itself out.

Although the fishing grounds around South Island are among the best the lake can offer, local fishermen obviously have a healthy appetite for goat meat. Over the years, almost all the feral goats have been killed for the pot or spirited away in small boats to the mainland.

Today, Lake Turkana is 160 miles long and between eight and twenty-seven miles wide. Covering a surface area of 2919 square miles, its mean depth is 103 feet with the deepest soundings at 374 feet recorded in the southern sector. Twenty-one per cent of the lake lies under thirty feet of water and explains the considerable changes to the shoreline this century. Because it has lain in a closed basin without any surface outflow for 6–8000 years, its waters contain sodium carbonate with a high level of fluoride. Though slippery to the touch and unpleasant to drink, in an emergency it will do one no harm. Tea does not make it more palatable; the brew turns black and revolting.

The communities living around the lake have become accustomed to drinking the water because there is rarely an alternative source close at hand. Some of them add camels' milk to it to improve the taste. While a minute amount of fluoride is good for healthy teeth, a very high level is detrimental. Count Teleki added tartaric acid to the water he drank and claimed it tasted better. A more recent innovation if one can afford it, is to pump the water into shallow pans on the floor of an enclosed greenhouse-type structure. In the extreme heat, pure water condenses on the inside of the glass roof and is channelled into clean containers.

About ninety per cent of the water flowing into the lake is discharged from the River Omo. The seasonal rivers of the Turkwell and the Kerio supply less than ten per cent between them. Since the evaporation rate is about ten feet per annum, and a rough balance is maintained between inflow and evaporation, an unrestricted flow of water from the Omo is absolutely vital to the lake's survival. If ever a major dam was built upstream in Ethiopia for hydroelectric power generation, the lake could become another Aral Sea. As it is, prolonged droughts made more severe by desiccating winds have dramatic short-term effects. They cause water levels to fluctuate more than any other lake of natural origin in the world. The level has been known to drop forty feet in a decade.

There is a barely perceptible build up of alkalinity in the lake water as the process of evaporation concentrates its salts. However, scientists have not detected any increase which will threaten life in the lake for centuries to come. The beautiful jade colour of the water in certain light occurs where large amounts of green algae with high chlorophyll concentrations develop in the open waters. It is especially noticeable at the southern end of the lake where there is no seasonal inflow. The colour is so unusual and in such contrast to the drab, lifeless surroundings that in the blazing sun of a calm day, it is a sight never to be forgotten. There is good reason for calling this awesome lake the Jade Sea.

Despite the water's alkalinity, hippos thrive and fish abound, particularly on the protected eastern shoreline where commercial fishing has been negligible. Until the early 1970s, the lake was unique in that it did not support an indigenous fishing industry, even though tilapia and Nile perch are excellent eating. The reasons for the lack of exploitation arose from the remoteness of the region and the fundamental opposition of most Turkana towards fishing. Only men of the Ng'ibochoros territorial section customarily practised subsistence fishing in the shallow waters using traditional baskets or harpoons.

The Sibiloi National Park was gazetted in 1972 to protect the flora and fauna along Lake Turkana's eastern shoreline north of Allia Bay. The park also safeguards the wildlife and valuable palaeontogical sites in an area covering 606 square miles inland. Many species of animals can be seen there. Long ago, elephants used to migrate from Marsabit Mountain in the wet season, but the last time one was seen at the lakeshore was more than half a century ago. When Count Teleki passed through the area fifty years previously, the whole place teemed with game. He shot numerous elephants and rhinos to feed his hungry porters, thus contributing in his own small way to their eventual disappearance from the lake region.

These days very few animals can be seen along the unprotected western shores of the lake. Large herds of topi once grazed the plains between Mount Lapur and Todenyang, but they have disappeared for ever. When people have to fight poverty in a land of recurrent droughts and hunger, it is inevitable they will take their toll of the wild animals. The Turkana have learnt not to be too fastidious about what they eat, especially meat.

LEFT: Four million years ago, Kanapoi was at the edge of a lake, and had lush vegetation. Today, Lake Turkana is thirty miles away, and the area is exceptionally desolate. In 1995, a new hominid species was discovered here, establishing that bipedalism and upright posture go back in time more than four million years.

ABOVE: Koobi Fora has the richest fossil beds in the world. Each year, the constant erosion by wind and rain exposes new finds in the ancient sediments. This partially exposed jaw bone belongs to a prehistoric hippo of which there were four distinct species living in the region at different times.

BELOW: Deposits of fossilized or petrified wood can be found all over the lake region. Mostly, they date back to early Miocene, seventeen million years ago, when the country was covered in tropical vegetation. Huge tree trunks of an unknown type of wood form one of the finest displays at Allia Bay. No trees of comparable size can be seen anywhere near the lake today.

An ancient cemetery with burial mounds situated near Lokori. It is known to the local people as *Ng'amoratung'a* (the people of stone). The site dates back to between 355 and 165 BC. There are several of them in Turkanaland.

LEFT: Incessant winds create beautiful curves and patterns in the sand dunes at Eliye Springs where doum palm trees thrive in the infertile soil.

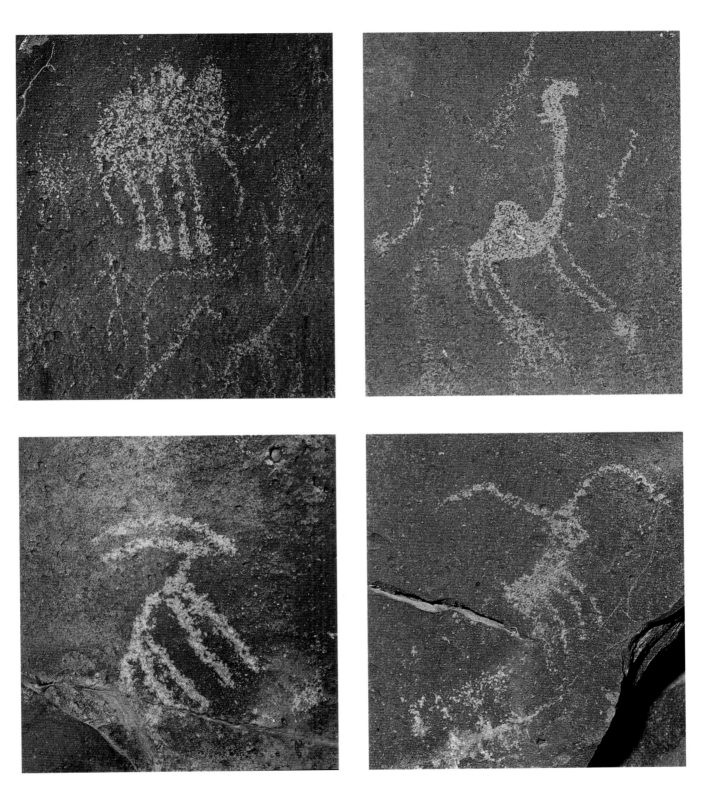

LEFT AND ABOVE: The largest site of primitive rock art, close to the remote southern end of Lake Turkana, was a chance discovery by Joy Adamson, author of *Born Free*, in 1944. The etchings are very beautiful depictions of men and animals resembling elephant, giraffe, oryx, camel and small gazelles cut about one to three millimetres deep in very hard basalt with no apparent effort to colour them. They show a more developed technique and a greater variety of subjects than other sites but their age is indeterminate. The settings for these notable displays are a number of deeply eroded river beds with steep sides of fractured boulders.

LEFT AND ABOVE: The Suguta Valley is a low-lying area of salt pans, mud flats and volcanic cones, surrounded by awesome mountain ranges. Once, a part of Lake Turkana, it has to be one of the hottest and most unpleasant corners of Kenya; a hell-on-earth where midday temperatures rise to 140° F in the shade, if you can find any. The nomads do not stay in the place for long, but they come for salt which is important for healthy stock.

Nestling among lava rocks beside the Suguta River are desert roses, *Adenium obesum*, which add a splash of colour to the arid regions. They are considered highly poisonous by most tribes but not so the Turkana who repeatedly boil the flowers, pods and roots for many hours before eating them.

RIGHT: *Suguta* means salt in the Turkana tongue. A river of the same name gushes from hot springs at Kapedo in the far south of Turkana district, then drops down an impressive waterfall before flowing north into the valley where it dissipates in the friable soil and heat. There is no other river in Kenya which is so saline; even livestock shun its clear, alluring waters.

The extinct volcano of Namurinyang typifies the volcanic origins of the Lake Turkana region. Situated in the searing heat of the Suguta Valley, it stands out pale from the inhospitable surroundings of black lava flows and reddish shale.

RIGHT: At the northern end of the Suguta Valley, Cathedral Rock is the rather grand name for a chunk of lava surrounded by Lake Lokipi. This 'lake' is a seasonal rainwater pan where lesser flamingos congregate when there is enough water for algae to grow. For much of the year it is bone dry.

A magnificent greater kudu bull. These antelopes inhabit the rocky hillsides and mountainous areas of the district. Their horns are used as warhorns by several tribes and blown to summon young men to arms but this has never been the practice among the Turkana.

LEFT: Rising from the Suguta Valley, the different coloured layers of exposed rock in these mountain ranges are a visible sign of intense volcanic activity millions of years ago. Grey-black, mauve and russet-brown basalt rock is scattered everywhere in chaotic profusion.

White-necked cormorants sun themselves on rocks at the foot of Porr, a prominent hill on the east side of Lake Turkana near El Molo Bay.

RIGHT: Protected from over-grazing since 1972, the Sibiloi National Park has better vegetation than other parts of the eastern side of Lake Turkana. Nevertheless, the lake's alkalinity limits the range of plant life that will grow close to the shoreline. The animal population in the park is varied and interesting. One hundred ago, elephants and rhinos inhabited the area, but they were poached out of existence in the early years of the twentieth century.

FOLLOWING PAGE: A mass of young Nile crocodiles. The marked decline in the crocodile population of Lake Turkana over the past ten years can be attributed to an increase in the human population. This has resulted in frequent disturbance by fishermen around their favoured basking and breeding areas. In any case, no man will tolerate for long wild creatures which swim invisibly through water and devour his family and livestock when they least suspect it.

The greater flamingo frequents all the alkaline lakes of the Great Rift Valley. It is graceful and very beautiful in flight, having bright coral-red wing coverts, axillaries and legs, and black flight feathers.

RIGHT: North Island is bleak and bare – a tiny island of compacted ash and precipitous cliffs. Sulphur jets are still active near the summit of the main cone. The very unpleasant feature of the place is its large population of poisonous snakes which include puff adders, vipers and spitting cobras; large rock pythons are also common. Not many people will spend a night there out of choice.

RIGHT AND ABOVE: Central Island is a National Park, famous for its crocodile breeding grounds and birdlife. It has two crater lakes of volcanic origin which are replenished from the main lake by underground seepage. Both have higher levels of conductivity than the waters of the lake, and are markedly different in colour. A third crater lake virtually dried up in 1976 after a mysterious midnight explosion fissured its bed and stunned all the fish; the fishermen reaped a bonanza that day! There are still signs of volcanic activity on the island.

South Island is Lake Turkana's largest island. Situated in the southern sector of the lake where the water reaches its maximum depth of 374 feet, the island is a spine of volcanic cones and hills covering an area of 15 square miles. The lava flows (*left*) are remarkably well preserved, and look of recent origin. In 1955, the island was the last part of the lake basin to be explored. Feral goats have roamed there for more than sixty years.

PRECEDING PAGES, LEFT, ABOVE AND FOLLOWING PAGES: The traditional fishing baskets of the Ng'ibochoros fishermen are conical in shape and made from pliable sticks and twisted palm fronds. They are between three and four feet wide at the mouth and have a small flap at the top of the cone. When there is no wind, groups of men either fish shortly before dawn, attracting the fish to their baskets with lighted faggots made from tight bundles of doum plam fronds, or at daybreak. They form a semicircle in the shallow waters about one hundred yards or so from land. Moving in concert toward the shore, they frequently plunge their baskets into the water to catch the encircled fish. When one is trapped, it is removed through the hole at the top of the basket and secured to a hand-held stick through its gills or trailed from a rope behind the fisherman who caught it. These traditional methods are not often used these days for the simple reason that small mesh gillnets were introduced some years ago resulting in a marked decline of fish in the shallow waters.

The Turkana spear-fish in the shallow lake waters. The wooden shaft has a detachable metal point and a sharp barb. This is secured to one end of a long piece of coiled rope, while the other end is usually tied around the fisherman's waist. I have watched for hours, fascinated by the skill of a man (*right*) who caught four tilapia and five barbel in an afternoon. Knee-deep in shallow water, he was extremely patient and unerringly accurate when he thrust his spear at a moving fish.

Traditional rafts (*above*) are often used in waist-deep water. These rudimentary craft are made by lashing four or five doum-palm logs together. Dugout canoes are uncommon because large trees do not grow in the vicinity of Lake Turkana.

ABOVE: Lake Turkana is host to forty-eight fish species of which ten are endemic. They tend to prove that the lake was connected to the Nile system as recently as 7000 years ago. The *Distichodus* fish has a distinctive bright yellow flesh and is found in places where fresh water enters the lake. A fisherman makes good use of his all-purpose wrist knife to fillet it.

RIGHT: A fisherman sun-dries his catch on lava rocks, which takes a day in the fierce heat. Tilapia are in great demand in Western Kenya. They are cut open and laid out flat to dry, whereas Nile perch, a much larger fish often weighing more than 100 lbs, are cut into strips.

FOLLOWING PAGES: A fisherman pulls his boat to safe harbour on the eastern shore of Lake Turkana. More and more conventional fishing boats are being used for offshore fishing within the fifty-foot contour. Most are owned by people from outside the district who bring planks and boatbuilders to the lake, and build their boats along the shore.

EPILOGUE

Few communities in the world could have been as successful as the Turkana in extracting a living from their harsh, unforgiving land. Outsiders do not begin to understand the level of sophistication that is required to keep body and soul together, and livestock healthy in conditions so overwhelmingly adverse. Visitors are acutely aware, however, that wind, heat, dust, and thirst quickly sap one's strength while myriad little flies which wake up with the sun and annoy all day, make life a perfect misery.

The Turkana are proud and independent yet have now reached a crossroads in our rapidly changing world and are unsure which way to turn. Their lives as expert stockmen have been affected by circumstances beyond their control, namely droughts exacerbated by man-made borders and cross-border raids. Pastoralists are the first to suffer whenever droughts occur. Though they have always loomed large in Turkanaland, incidences of prolonged dry periods are worsening, just as they are throughout the Sahel where the desert encroaches inexorably. Global warming is said to be the major cause although the Turkana have no doubt in their own minds where the fault lies. The old men will explain that droughts only became a serious problem after the coming of the white man; it is they who are responsible for their plight!

Cross-border raids have had a devastating effect on people's lives. Homesteads in the remote areas are terrorized, innocent people killed, livestock stolen at gun-point and large tracts of good grazing lie fallow because the predatory aspirations of gun-toting neighbours make them too dangerous to use. The ideal of border tribes peacefully coexisting is still unrealistic when hate, fear and suspicion can best describe their relations with each other for longer than anyone can remember. Those who brave the border regions live on a war footing in constant fear of attack.

The Turkana do have a well-deserved reputation as a fighting race and are not blameless. Their well-armed, lawless bands, called *ng'oroko*, roam the countryside, and are unpredictable and ruthless. At times they defend their own people against attack; at other times they rob them of a few animals to feed themselves. Everybody tolerates the *ng'oroko* but nobody likes them because they have no compunction about killing law-abiding citizens who report their activities. Nevertheless, the *ng'oroko* have not been the underlying cause of strife in the last twenty years. The trouble started way back in 1979 when the Karamojong raided the Uganda Army barracks at Moroto and looted the armoury during the anarchy which followed the overthrow of the infamous dictator, Idi Amin.

Drought and insecurity have resulted in hunger and an undue reliance on food aid. Up to one third of all Turkana families have lost their livestock and are miserably poor, living a bare subsistence life. In the inhospitable terrain of Turkanaland, once a person has nothing, it is virtually impossible for him to ever get anything again. Unfortunately, few aid organizations look beyond provisioning food because it is cheaper to dump the world's surplus on the starving than to store it. The few agencies which are concerned about a solution, realize the Turkana have to be helped to become self-reliant again. They also understand the value of restocking programmes because the most efficient way of producing food in the arid north is still by tending livestock.

There is another aspect to hunger which cannot be ignored. The population has more than tripled in forty years which has outstripped the natural increase of the herds and the carrying capacity of the land. Unless

LEFT: A lifetime of drinking the waters of Lake Turkana, which contain sodium carbonate with a high level of fluoride, has left this old man with severely deformed joints. Teeth also discolour and eventually rot.

Mission crucifixes make ideal ornaments.

measures are taken to persuade the nomads to have fewer children, they will become steadily poorer and the future will be bleak. This is problematic in a society that still counts wealth in terms of cattle and the number of women a man marries, and where children are perceived as an insurance against old age. No matter what, a solution has to be found to reverse this trend. As a generalization, a population density of fifteen per square mile in an arid country like Turkana district is sustainable before a potentially catastrophic condition has to be resolved by conflict, famine or emigration. Nowadays, as a result of international food aid, people are unlikely to starve to death. For better or worse, nature's way of correcting a chronic imbalance has been eliminated. Ultimately, this will increase the chances of conflict.

Turkana district has been a favourite target for the aid industry. As early as 1961, The district commissioner described his district as 'a pit into which money must always be thrown without any return'. Since then, aid money has been poured into the district with little to show for it. A fish processing factory, fish ponds for breeding tilapia to replenish the lake's dwindling resources, and large scale irrigation schemes have been funded by international donors and failed. Seemingly, they were all too reliant on massive capital input, skills, machinery, and spares from elsewhere. The biggest disaster was the fish factory. Had the Turkana been consulted, they would have told the donors in their forthright manner that the whole concept of freezing fresh fish fillets was unnecessary. They had no problem selling their catches. Sun-dried, salted fish were exported to Zaire while a ready market existed for smoked fish in Western Kenya. The trade was simple and straightforward with no waste. The high-tech project merely encouraged excess harvesting by fishermen who flocked to Lake Turkana from other parts of Kenya, and succeeded in making the Turkana, who fished by traditional means, much worse off.

The Turkana need projects and practical assistance that will improve their lifestyle, not change it. They also need to be involved in the decision-making processes at grassroots level because schemes imposed on them are bound to fail. Affluent societies pity the nomads and want to improve their lot by turning them into settled communities. However, nomadism is an age-old pursuit and the only effective means of utilizing marginal land. The Turkana value their freedom and untrammelled existence. They live for their livestock which will perish if they do not follow the rains.

The Catholic church responded to the people's needs in a very practical way. Finance was raised to start the 'Turkana Water Project' which resulted in the installation of boreholes and fifty hand-operated water pumps. Nothing could have been more welcome to people living in an arid area where water is seldom within easy reach of their transient homesteads. The success of the project was in part due to the deliberate involvement of local communities in site selection, construction of access roads, and providing pump attendants.

The church has also been a driving force in educating the Turkana even though nomadism makes schooling

Water pumps — a boon to all in arid lands.

awkward and contributed to a complete lack of facilities in the district until 1960. Therefore, few adults in the remote areas speak Ki-swahili, the lingua franca of East Africa. It is already evident that the disadvantaged, stockless families have more educated children than the pastoral communities whose numbers must always be large enough to cope with the workload. This could be changed by a more imaginative approach to education with teachers accompanying nomadic communities, and giving children lessons in their transitory homes. Although the curriculum would have to be adapted to the special needs of nomadic children by emphasizing animal husbandry, health, and veterinary subjects, members of a new generation would be better equipped to uplift the living standards of their own people with girls improving hygiene and health in the home. This novel concept might reduce the drift of educated children to urban centres where the majority fail to find employment, yet are reluctant to return home and resume a productive, albeit traditional, way of life.

We live in an era of unstoppable change, and the Turkana cannot be left in a vacuum. A transition to different circumstances is as inevitable as it is welcome providing their quality of life improves. It has taken the Turkana hundreds of years to evolve a unique lifestyle to suit their hostile environment, and considerable care has to be taken to ensure that new development ideas are in tune with their needs. Putting these ideas into practice is much easier said than done when dealing with supremely confident, almost arrogant, people who are not easily persuaded to embrace change. Their most pressing need is to rid their district of banditry. Without peace and stability, there can be little progress or prosperity.

Many old men look back nostalgically to the time when their forefathers reigned supreme and regret the day their expansion was stopped by the barrel of the gun. Had their movement south not been checked by the British, they might have become the largest stock and landowners in Kenya. Since the power of the Maasai was already in decline in the 1880s due to debilitating internecine wars, their defeat by the Turkana would have been inevitable. Anyway, the Turkana considered Maasai warriors effeminate, for they sat on the ground like their women, rather than on stools!

I have attempted to record in this book some of the fascinating customs and traditions of the Turkana before it is too late. When pastoralists lose their livestock and come under sustained pressure, their lifestyles are transformed; in the process, customs change or are lost for ever. This is now becoming more and more apparent in Turkanaland. Despite the Turkana's respect for nature and land in which they live, their struggle against the odds is almost overwhelming.

I have travelled more than 25,000 miles in my Land-Rover during the past four years, much of it on appalling tracks and to the remote corners of the district. I have had my fair share of excitements and disappointments, yet my experiences have not changed my admiration and respect for a people who are so resolute in adversity.

SELECT BIBLIOGRAPHY

Austin, H. H., *Among Swamps and Giants in Equatorial Africa* (London, 1902)

Austin, H. H., *With Macdonald in Uganda* (London, 1903)

Barber, J. P., *Imperial Frontier* (Nairobi, 1967)

Barber, J. P., 'The Macdonald Expedition to the Nile 1897–1899' (Uganda Journal, 1964)

Barrett,Anthony, *Dying and death among the Turkana* (Nairobi, 1987)

Barton, Juxon, 'Notes on the Turkana Tribe of British East Africa', Parts I & II
(*Journal of the African Society*, 1920/1921)

Beachey, R. W., 'The arms Trade in East Africa in the late Nineteenth Century'
(*Journal of African History*, 1962)

Collins, R. O., 'The Turkana Patrol, 1918' (*Uganda Journal*, 1961)

Eliot, Sir Charles, *The British East African Protectorate*, (London, 1905)

Good, James, *Mission to Turkana* (Midleton, Co.Cork, 1988)

Graham, Alistair, and Beard, Peter, *Eyelids of the Morning* (Greenwich, USA, 1973)

Gulliver, P. H., *A Preliminary Survey of the Turkana* (University of Cape Town, 1950)

Gulliver, P. H. and Pamela, *The Central Nilo-Hamites* (International African Institute, 1953)

Höhnel, L. von, *Discovery of Lakes Rudolf and Stefanie*, Vol. II (London, 1894)

Höhnel, L. von, 'The Lake Rudolf Region: Its Discovery and Subsequent Exploration, 1888–1909'
(*Journal of the African Society*, 1938)

Hopson, A. J. (ed), *A Report on the Findings of the Lake Turkana Project* 1972–1975 (London, 1982)

Johnston, Sir Harry, *The Uganda Protectorate* (London, 1902)

Lamphear, John, *The Scattering Time* (Oxford, 1992)

Lamphear, John, 'The People of the Grey Bull: The Origin and Expansion of the Turkana'
(*Journal of African History*, 1988)

Moyse-Bartlett, H., *The King's African Rifles* (Aldershot,1956)

Powell Cotton, P. H. G., *In Unknown Africa* (London, 1904)

Rayne, H. H., *The Ivory Raiders* (London, 1923)

Rayne, H. H., 'Turkana Parts I and II' (*Journal of the African Society*, 1919)

Soper, R. C. (ed), *Socio-Cultural Profile of Turkana District* (Nairobi, n.d.)

RIGHT: A girl hurries home over windswept dunes as long shadows cast by the setting sun herald the end of another scorching day.

FOLLOWING PAGE: The welfare of his stock is a man's overriding concern. As darkness falls, an elder watches his animals driven into the stock pens for the night. He will instantly know if one is missing by his ability to picture every animal in his mind.